Emily

WOMEN IN THE WEST

Series editors:

Sandra L. Myres
University of Texas at
Arlington

Elliott West
of Arkansas

:ffrey
ollege

University of Nebraska Press: Lincoln and London

Emily

The Diary of a Hard-Worked Woman

By Emily French

Edited by

Janet Lecompte

The paper in this book meets the
minimum requirements
of American National Standard for
Information Sciences –
Permanence of Paper for Printed
Library Materials
ANSI Z39.48-1984.

Library of Congress Cataloging
in Publication Data
French, Emily, b. ca. 1843.
Emily, the diary
of a hard-worked woman.
(Women in the West)
Bibliography: p.
Includes index.
1. French, Emily, b. ca. 1843 –
Diaries. 2. Pioneers –
Colorado – Diaries. 3. Women
pioneers – Colorado –
Diaries. 4. Working class women –
Colorado – Diaries.
5. Colorado – Social life and
customs. I. Lecompte,
Janet, 1923- . II. Title.
III. Title: Emily. IV. series.
F781.F854 1987
978.8'031'0924 [B] 86-11389
ISBN 0-8032-2872-4 (alk. paper)
ISBN 0-8032-6861-0 (pbk.: alk. paper)

Contents

Preface

Diaries of day laborers describing their work are hard to come by. Some were illiterate, some were ill, some were too poor, or too tired, or too busy to keep journals. Their work was ordinary, dull, routine; most workers were probably not very interested in their work.

Emily French was a laundress, cleaning woman, and nurse, and she was interested in her work. She was often busy, tired, or ill, but she faithfully kept a diary that is remarkable in its description of her work and how she felt about it. She was equally articulate about other aspects of her life, such as her family, friends, horses, activities, clothes, values, and God. Through this expressive diary we can feel Emily's pain and her rare moments of joy, and we experience what it was like to be a poor working woman in Colorado in 1890.

Emily French's diary, a brown cloth-covered book of 3 by 5 inches, is worn but sturdy, like Emily herself. Although Emily once dropped it into a pail of water, its pages are still clean and her small penciled script is still legible. The first printed pages contain a miscellany of useful facts, such as phases of the moon, current interest rates (4 percent to 6 percent), and common wages ($3 to $24 for a six-day, sixty-hour week). The diary itself provides a blank page for each day, headed by a printed date and day of the week. The last pages are printed with headings for "Letter Register," "Visits," "Memoranda," and "Cash Account." I have added

Emily's sparse entries under "Letter Register" and "Visits" to the body of the diary of corresponding date.

To help the reader make sense out of this dense and compressed diary, I have provided a general introduction giving what I know of Emily's previous circumstances and a context for events described in the diary; I have provided short introductions to the four sections of the diary; I have supplied endnotes identifying sources and adding relevant material; and I have collected in an epilogue what little is known of Emily and her family after the diary ends.

Emily usually omitted punctuation, and the manuscript diary is difficult to understand for that reason. To make the diary readable, I have added commas and periods, but nothing more—dashes or exclamation points in the diary are Emily's. The religious quotations at the beginning of the entries were spread over the head of two facing pages of the diary; for the sake of coherence I have put these quotations at the head of the first page on which they appear. I have not noted Emily's marginal additions unless the fact that they were marginal changed her emphasis. Otherwise I have not tinkered with the text.

I am especially indebted to Catherine and Donald Jackson, who did research on the French family in Anamosa, Iowa, and to George Davenport who performed the same service in Storm Lake, Iowa; to Sandra Myres, whose interest and excellent editing has been all-important; to Elizabeth Hampsten, Julie Roy Jeffrey, Elliott West, and Judith Gamble, who read the manuscript and made valuable comments; to Carol Hilgendorf of the Elbert County Library in Kiowa, Colorado; to Glenn R. Scott who provided me with references to Morgan Rood; to Rosemary Hetzler of the Pioneers' Museum, Colorado Springs; to Mary Davis of the Penrose Public Library, Colorado Springs; to Kay Engle and staff of the Stephen Hart Library at the Colorado Historical Society; and to the staffs of Western History in the Denver Public Library, the Colorado State Archives, and the many other libraries and offices. And not least, to Barbara Neilon, George Fagan, John Sheridan, and the Tutt Library at The Colorado College, for preserving and locating the diary and for giving me permission to publish it.

JANET LECOMPTE

Discovering Emily

Jan. 1st 1890. Emily L. French. Elbert Colorado. Let me only in the fear of God put on these pages what shall transpire in my poor life. Pure truths are only of value. I seek not the aplause of the people, only that I may deserve the epitaph—She hath done what she could.

Thus Emily French states her objectives for her diary, and her humble goals for her life. "Pure truths only," often set down in painful intensity, are the stuff of this diary. We see Emily as though naked before God, with all her prejudices, impulsiveness, anger, and self-pity, as well as her courage, generosity, and strength.

Her "pure truths" are not typical of the genre. In a study of midwestern women's diaries from 1880 to 1910, Elizabeth Hampsten concludes that women diarists and letter writers valued success, achievement, and optimism, the ingredients of the era's much-prized "progress." As a consequence, women consistently denied any stress or failure, maintaining a facade of assurance and serenity in their writings, even in the face of personal disaster.[1]

Emily's diary was her trusted confidante, "this dear and only friend I seem to have" (August 31), "the holder of my poor thoughts and actions" (March 30) that "I shall love to read in the future" (April 24). These are her stated reasons for keeping a diary, but the astute reader might guess that a need for self-expression and love of writing also motivated her.[2] She expresses her emotions so spontaneously that the reader is seldom in doubt about what she is feeling. She shapes her dramatic encounters using a few words to produce vivid and immediate scenes such as this description of a Mauck family quarrel:

Morrice he began to scream, his father took him, she bounded as quick as lightning across the kitchen, hit the child a slap on the head, the father put it down, went over to her, hit her, then she run out of the room, the baby left screaming (November 7).

In 1890 Emily French was forty-seven years old. Her hands were gnarled from years of housework and rough from daily contact with strong soap and harsh water; she called herself "a hard worked woman" (August 25). Her hair was graying, her shoulders were bent, she wore gold eyeglasses, and her teeth were false—so her diary describes her (January 20, February 27, March 30, May 2). She was not unattractive, however. Three bachelors came to see her with a persistence she claimed not to understand, until one of them proposed marriage.

Emily Louisa Rood was born near the town of Marshall, Calhoun County, Michigan, on August 14, 1843 (August 14), one of at least four children of Morgan L. Rood and his first wife, whose name is unknown. In 1848 Morgan Rood went to California and returned to Michigan with a reputed $10,000 in gold dust. He followed the gold miners again in 1859, this time leaving his family for good to settle in Denver where he established a successful gun shop. Rood and Emily's mother were apparently divorced; he married Mrs. Anna Bickford in Denver in 1868, and lived with her in prosperous circumstances until his death in November 1881.[3]

On March 17, 1858, Emily eloped with Marsena H. French from New York State, and was married in Calhoun County, Michigan. Emily was fifteen; Marsena was twenty-three. Their first child, Ada, was born in Michigan in 1860; their next six children were born in Iowa: Helen H. in 1862, Marsena B. in 1864, Emily A. in 1867, Chauncey Morgan (later Morgan Chauncey) in 1869, Abigail M. in 1871, Olive Esther in 1875. By 1865 they were living in eastern Iowa at Anamosa, a pretty town of 2,000 people where Marsena worked as a clerk in a clothing store. In

March 1867, he bought the store from its owner and began his own clothing business. That year he served as city councilman.[4]

For the next two years Marsena spent much of his time away from Anamosa, apparently in medical school. Emily was not badly off then; the 1870 census shows that her occupation was "keeping house," and that in her own name she had $800 worth of real estate and $100 worth of personal property. In April 1870, Marsena announced in the newspaper that he was prepared to give his undivided attention to the practice of medicine in Anamosa and vicinity. The editor of the newspaper assured readers that Dr. French was competent and trustworthy, "having already had considerable experience and careful preparation" as a doctor. In the meantime his clothing business had failed, and he filed for bankruptcy in Dubuque, Iowa, in May 1870.[5]

Five months after beginning his practice in Anamosa, Marsena went to Chicago to take a course of lectures.[6] By this time he had probably acquired more medical education than the average doctor of that day, when few doctors received formal training or were licensed. The practice of medicine was not yet a lucrative and respected profession. A young doctor in the first five years of practice often made less than $15 a month in cash, and nearly half of all doctors earned less than $2,000 a year. In an age when treatment was of limited effectiveness, a successful doctor sought to establish himself in a community and develop his social connections. Marsena seems to have failed in that respect.[7]

By September 1871 the French family had moved to Newell, a village in western Iowa near Storm Lake, where Marsena practiced medicine. In April 1874 they moved into Storm Lake, and the next year, according to the *Storm Lake Pilot,* they built a "fine residence" near the lake. Here Emily gave birth to Olive (Ollie) in July 1875.[8]

In the spring of 1876 the family moved to Golden, Colorado, a coal and railroad town at the foot of the mountains 12 miles west of Denver. Marsena practiced medicine here but made little money, for Emily now "worked out" for other families (July 18). In October 1877 she gave birth to Daniel T. French. By 1880 they had returned to Iowa and were living in Troy Mills, Linn County, 30 miles up the Wapsie River from Anamosa.[9]

Before 1881 Emily gave birth to her last child, M. K. French, Jr., in Iowa, and by 1882 the family had moved to Denver. In November 1881, Emily's father, Morgan L. Rood, had died in Denver, leaving to his second wife what was then a sizable estate estimated at $15,000 in real estate and $15,000 in personal property. Rood's children, Emily French, John Rood, Isaac Rood, and Annis Rood, sued for a share of the estate, and lost their case. According to the diary, the small amount remaining for Emily and Annis was entrusted to Oliver B. Liddell, a respected Denver attorney and district judge, who continued to lend or give Emily money after the trust was depleted.[10]

During the litigation the Frenches lived in Denver. A month before their claim to Rood's estate was denied in June 1884, they had taken up a dryland farm on the plains 3 miles east of Elbert, Colorado. Marsena spent over a year developing their 160 acres, building a house and outbuildings, and ploughing and planting. In the fall of 1885 when the crops were harvested, Marsena advertised his intention to resume medical practice in Elbert, and part-time practice at Franceville, a coal-mining town 30 miles southwest of Elbert, just east of Colorado Springs.[11]

In 1884 Emily's younger sister Annis Rood came to live in Colorado, and to take up a homestead adjoining Marsena's and Emily's. Annis was born in 1847 in Calhoun County, Michigan. By 1870 she was living in Hammonton, New Jersey, with the family of a tailor named Warren Samson. In 1870 Annis fell down the stairs at Hammonton and injured her spine. From that time on, she could not stand erect and had to be carried up stairs and into buggies. She was not so disabled, however, that she could not live alone on her Colorado homestead from July 1884 until 1890. When she later lived with Emily she helped by cooking, making fires, knitting stockings, making rugs and quilts, and reading out loud. Emily's feelings about Annis alternated between pity and resentment, but her concern for her never wavered.[12]

Marsena and Annis filed on their contiguous homesteads in May 1885. Annis's house, barn, and other buildings were on Marsena's land, apparently because Annis's land had no water (January 5). The French homestead had a four-room frame house and other improvements, including stables, wells, a corral, outbuildings,

fencing, and 18 acres ploughed. Marsena also filed on an adjacent
quarter-section under the Timber Culture Act requiring 10 acres
planted to trees. From 1887 to 1890 Chauncey and Abigail French
helped their father plant tree seeds, as they later testified, and their
testimony helped Marsena secure the land even though the little
trees all died from drought or frost.[13]

When Marsena and Annis took up their land, farming without
irrigation on the high plains of Colorado was profitable. In the
spring of 1885, ample and timely rainfall caused dryland farms to
produce good crops of corn, oats, alfalfa, and potatoes, and farmers flocked to the high plains of Colorado. Newspapers began call-
ing eastern Colorado "the rain belt"; myths about rain following
the plough and trees attracting rainfall brought more dryland
farmers, as well as promoters and speculators. Then the rains
ceased. In 1889 and 1890 a severe drought desiccated the eastern
plains. Thousands of ruined farmers and those dependent upon
their trade, like Emily French, went to the cities seeking work.[14]

In October 1887 Marsena returned to Iowa for a year, "on business" as he later testified. After he returned (or perhaps before he
left) Emily and Marsena were estranged, and Marsena filed for divorce. In December 1888, both Annis and Emily made wills re-
voking previous wills in which Marsena was beneficiary. Emily's
diary tells us that "the old rascal" French cheated Annis and her of
$1,000 each, but she does not say how he did it (January 13). Mar-
sena was granted a divorce in Denver on June 29, 1889, after a
marriage of thirty-one years.[15]

Emily wrote in her diary that Marsena "is an awful mean old
fellow, I never knew so until now, I used to think even he was
good" (February 22). Notices of Marsena in the Anamosa and
Storm Lake newspapers indicate that he was intelligent and per-
sonable. But his unsuccessful practice as a physician, his frequent
failures, absences, and moves, as well as evidence in Emily's diary,
show that he had a problem with alcohol. There were other
strains on the marriage, such as Marsena's inability to support his
family as a physician; the death of their four-year-old son, M. K.
French, Jr., in 1885 by accidental poisoning; and their frustration
at the outcome of the litigation over Morgan Rood's estate. The
immediate cause of the divorce may have been, in that durable

platitude, the "other woman." Shortly after Marsena was granted his divorce, he married Celia Firman of Iowa and brought her and her six-year-old son to the Colorado homestead. In September 1890, Celia gave birth to Marsena's son, Charles Dewitt French.[16]

The divorce was the climax of ruptured relationships in the French and Rood families that began years before the date of the diary. As late as 1881 Morgan Rood's widow thought Emily was still living in Anamosa, where in fact she had not lived for nine years, suggesting that when Emily lived in Golden she did not visit her father in Denver only 12 miles away. Emily seems to have been alienated from most of her own children. She did not know whether her daughter Emily, now twenty-three, was alive or dead (May 23); she declared her daughter Abigail to have lost all shame (December 9) and to have forgotten her (March 2); her eldest daughter Ada was "poor Ada," without further explanation (May 10); Helen and Marsena B. French are not mentioned in the diary; and she testified against her son Chauncey in Annis's suit for theft of a $25 harness. The family was split in two. Abigail (married to Sam Mellor) and Chauncey lived with Marsena and his new family on the homestead, while Emily was hiding the two youngest children, Ollie and Dannie in a boarding house in Denver and sending letters to them via an intermediary, Addie Quick (January 17).[17]

When the diary opens, Emily has just returned from Denver to Elbert, mainly to secure Annis's homestead by moving her house and other buildings from Marsena's to Annis's land. Emily supported Annis, Ollie, and Dannie by doing housework for her neighbors. In Elbert in 1890 Emily was never out of work, in spite of the economic crisis caused by the drought. She may have been the only woman in town "working out," and probably she could have found no other kind of work. The only Elbert businesses advertising in the *Colorado Business Directory* for 1890 were a family-operated restaurant, a general store, a lumber business, a small hotel, and a man who sold real estate and secondhand goods.[18]

Emily and Annis lived in a house rented from Mary Frick. Emily worked for the Fricks and the Oaks, the prosperous families of Elbert, and for the Baltzells and Sloans, who were nearly as poor as she was. Her employers were her friends; they helped her at work, and sent her home with food and clothing. But money was scarce in Elbert, and she was paid less often in cash than in house rent, fodder for her horse, hot meals, and kindness. Emily was eager to leave Elbert, where she was sick much of the winter. She yearned for her two children in Denver, was uncomfortable around Marsena and his supporters in Elbert, and could not accumulate any money.[19]

In the spring of 1890 Emily got Annis settled on her homestead, and then she moved to Denver. For a while she lived in the Larkin house where her children had spent the winter, and she enjoyed herself. She visited old friends, attended big public celebrations, built a house, and fell in love.[20]

In May 1890, Emily began to build a house, a four-room story-and-a-half frame house that was not quite finished at the end of the year. She could not afford a well; she used the polluted waters of the South Platte River half a block east for household needs and for watering her horse. The cost of the lot and house left her destitute. When she tried to find a job in Denver, there was none.[21]

To pay her debts she went to work in the mountains, first at a resort hotel at Buffalo Creek Park, and finally at Dake, a tiny mountain town.[22] In Dake Emily tried to make some money doing laundry and mending for Dake's transient and unstable population, but she barely made her expenses. Her joy at being hired as a nurse for a new mother and baby turned to despair after she massaged the mother's breasts to help the baby nurse, and was criticized and scorned for it (August 19).

Emily returned to Denver to face a cold winter in her unfinished house. She worked a week for the carping Mrs. Burnham, and two months for the abusive Mrs. Mauck. Then she paid a visit to Elbert. In Elbert her first business was preparing Annis's homestead for final proof of occupancy. Her second business was to appear in the Elbert County courthouse at Kiowa, Colorado, to testify against Chauncey and Marsena French on Annis's charges of theft of a harness. The charges against Marsena were dropped; a jury found Chauncey not guilty. Emily says nothing in the diary about the charges or verdict, for her concern was collecting witness fees. By this time her need for money outweighed nearly everything else in her life, except for her fear of losing Dannie. To Emily's distress, Chauncey had invited Dannie to visit him in Barr City north of Denver.[23] After Christmas Dannie ran away, and Emily was distraught. On New Year's Eve he returned, and she wrote, "Oh here is Dannie," the last and perhaps happiest words of the diary. She had survived 1890, a year of frustration and anguish, and had managed to hold on to what she valued—her own respectability, and her little family.

Emily was often dependent upon the generosity of a few kind neighbors to keep her going, for in the Victorian era little public aid was offered to the poor. Most poor people were thought to have brought their misfortunes upon themselves and were thus "undeserving." No public welfare eased workers' periods of unemployment or illness, and private charitable organizations gave small amounts of financial aid only to "deserving" applicants, such as respectable women and their children in temporary want.[24]

Although Emily never refers to her childhood in her diary, she had obviously been brought up with middle-class manners and values, and expectations of having "nice things" such as a horse and buggy, silk dresses, and a house of her own. She had absorbed the principles of the "cult of domesticity," in which women were submissive to their husbands except in matters of morals and spirituality, which became "woman's sphere." "True" women were pious and pure, and their place was in the home and in the church. In their limited world apart from the daily lives of men, "true" women formed deep friendships with other women.[25]

Emily could not practice all the principles of "true womanhood" after divorce deprived her of a husband's support, and the need to work out deprived her of a settled home life. She seems to have invested "home" and "church" with a transcendent significance when her hold on these sacred locales faltered. The word "home" appears with frequency and emphasis in the diary. "Home" probably meant to Emily all that she had lost, not only love, marriage, and family, but also security, reputation, and self-esteem. Similarly, church meant more to Emily than a house of worship. Although her faith in God was a strong and private source of strength, her church served a further function as a social equalizer where she was the peer of all other Christians, or at least Baptists.

In accordance with "true womanhood," most of Emily's friends were women, some of them "true," like Mrs. Corbin, and some not, like the devious, street-wise Luella Larkin. Emily needed her women friends for more than moral support after her divorce; by 1890 she was dependent upon them for money and food. Her judgments about their husbands were mostly negative and even hostile. The few she liked were family men, devoted to home and church, highly moral, affectionate, and sober.

Emily's standards of male behavior were common for the era, as Robert L. Griswold shows in his study of family and divorce in California. By 1880 husbands who acted as stern patriarchs toward their submissive wives and children were no longer admired. The ideal marriage had become increasingly one of mutual respect, kindness, and affection. Married couples now had higher expectations of each other, not only as providers and housekeepers, but also as lovers and companions. These needs were more complex and difficult to meet, and divorce increased accordingly—fourfold in the United States between 1860 and 1900.[26]

Emily's divorce freed her from her husband's jurisdiction, but it deprived her of any financial help from him, for she received no alimony or child support. As a divorced woman, Emily did not suffer the degree of disgrace her mother must have experienced thirty years earlier. By 1890 at least 3 in every 1,000 marriages ended in divorce, and in western states the incidence of divorce was even higher, according to government statistics. Government statistics on divorce were very conservative; an 1880 article in the *North American Review* estimated one divorce to every 8.1 marriages in Connecticut, and one to every 14.8 marriages in Massachusetts. In some years the divorce rate multiplied five times as fast as the population increase, especially among the lower classes where half the widows and divorced women worked away from the home. In short, divorce was still a stigma for a woman in 1890, but too common to be a social disaster.[27]

Divorce was just one aspect of the retreat of "true womanhood." By 1890 women of all classes were rejecting the old feminine virtues and making "outrageous" demands. They wanted the vote, the end of the double standard of sexual behavior, and the right to work at men's jobs (in 1850 the United States had no women doctors; in 1890 there were 2,000). Women even showed up in men's clothing—the "abominable new fashions" for women included blazers, cravats, cutaway coats, and sailor hats.[28]

Emily tried to maintain the old standards of modest, decorous, genteel behavior, even though she showed a more aggressive mien in her dealings with rough men in the building trades. Above all she fought to maintain her reputation for decency. People assumed that a female servant was not much better than a whore, and in fact this was often so. An investigation of prostitution at the end of the century showed that about a third of the women "in service" in homes, hotels, or restaurants, were forced by low wages to become prostitutes. The common assumption of the era that working women had loose morals—and the fact that Emily was divorced—was probably what caused Mrs. Mauck to call her an "adventuress" (October 29).[29]

In 1890 Emily French was one of many thousand single working women in Denver, where jobs were hard to get. In 1890 the average working woman in the United States had started to work at age fifteen and was now twenty-two, earning less than $6 a week for a twelve-hour day. The single working woman of Denver would have envied this twenty-two-year-old statistic for her steady job. In Denver 15 percent of all women worked in 1890, most of them as domestics, laundresses, or seamstresses, some making as much as $4 to $6 a week. In 1890 half the nation's widows and divorced women were employed, but in Denver fewer than a third worked because of the lack of jobs. Unlike eastern cities, Denver had almost no factories or mills; one of the few was A. Z. Solomon's sweatshop where Emily worked for a week making men's suits; she called it "awful" work (September 22).[30]

Very often Emily did not make $4 to $6 a week. In Elbert she charged a dollar a day for housecleaning and washing, more for ironing and mending, but she earned (if her accounts are accurate) $7.75 in cash for the month of January, $3.00 in February, and $9.00 in March. In Denver she worked less than in Elbert, and appeared to have earned less, although her accounts for the last half of the year are fragmentary. She was offered $35 dollars a month as cook at the Buffalo Creek Park resort hotel, but the highest steady wage she earned in Denver in 1890 was $20 a month as housekeeper for the Maucks. She considered this a fair wage, and she endured the job in spite of its irritations.

Emily's occupation was not really a matter of choice. Had she been younger she might have applied for a job as a waitress, country schoolteacher, or clerk in a store, but employers chose young, single women for these positions. Had she been trained she could have been a stenographer or hospital nurse; had she been educated she might even have been one of the 2,000 women physicians in the country. But her age and lack of skills, except in keeping house and raising children, determined her line of work.[31]

Nursing, in 1890 more often a household skill than a profession, was Emily's preferred occupation. "Nurse" was how she described herself in the Denver city directories of 1890 and 1891. She may have learned a little doctoring (and a few medical terms that turn up in the diary) as she helped her doctor-husband with his patients, but she probably had no formal training. Most of her patients were sick or postpartum women, and there were a lot of them. Invalidism of women in the nineteenth century was so widespread as to defy purely medical explanations. Scholars have attributed women's sickly constitutions to social causes, saying that ill health was a psychological reaction to the restrictions of woman's "place"; or that doctors encouraged women's ill health to keep them in their "place"; or that women feigned illness to gain sympathy or avoid responsibility. Historians have assumed that most invalids were middle-class or upper-class women, but Robert L. Griswold's statistics from California divorce cases indicate that over 40 percent of wives of men in menial jobs reported ill health, mostly "nervous" problems, a "delicate" constitution, or uterine disorders.[32] Many of the sick women and their families that Emily saw had ailments peculiar to poverty and lack of sanitation—diarrhea from polluted water, worms in children, bedbugs, lice, scabs on old scalps, impetigo on babies' faces. Emily herself was relatively healthy, as was her attitude about illness— the rich went to bed with it, the poor went to work.

Emily was always looking out for more pleasant and lucrative occupations. In February 1890, she applied to be an agent for a mail-order book company in Saint Louis ("so I need not wash"). Newspaper advertisements lured agents with promises of making thousands of dollars. Emily sent in her dollar for her "outfit" and managed to sell some but not enough books; in June she gave up the book business. At one point she considered taking in boarders, a common means of support for Denver's working women in 1890, but nothing came of it.[33]

Like most women of that era, Emily had not finished high school, having eloped at the age of fifteen from a family that was then or later broken by divorce. Her daughter Ollie did not finish high school, either, and also married at fifteen after a period of drudgery and abuse as a housemaid in Denver. Fifteen was not considered too early to start working. When Emily herself was a child, children as young as six years old were employed in the cloth mills of New England working fourteen to sixteen hours a day for wages of $1.50 a week. Working conditions for children gradually improved. In 1887 Colorado passed a law that no children under fourteen should work in mines, smelters, mills, or factories, but children who worked on farms or in houses were not restricted. Nor were they required to go to school. The first compulsory education law was passed in Illinois in 1883, requiring children between eight and fourteen to attend school for not less than twelve weeks a year. Compulsory school attendance was not generally favored until after the turn of the century.[34] So Emily felt no remorse in trying to find employment for thirteen-year-old Dannie, or in taking Ollie out of school to work in order to help pay for the house.

Emily's diary is an account of her attempt to "live well" in spite of difficult circumstances. During the year 1890 Emily had slipped from genteel poverty in a small supportive community to near starvation in a city indifferent to its poor. Emily's employers worked alongside her in Elbert where houseworkers were scarce; in Denver where houseworkers were common, Emily and her work were despised by many of her employers. Poverty was the matrix of her life in 1890, and the source of constant anxiety. But her deepest fears were centered, in this first full year after her divorce, on loss of family and of "home." Her expression of these fears becomes the most poignant part of this most expressive diary.

Elbert

The Plains in Winter

*Elbert, population 1,856 in 1890, was on the eastern plains of Colorado
50 miles southeast of Denver and 30 miles northeast of Colorado Springs.
It was a quiet ranching, farming, and lumbering center set in a grassy valley between pine-covered bluffs at the headwaters of West Kiowa Creek.*

*Like a thousand other western towns, Elbert's businesses and houses
were strung along both sides of a railroad track. Elbert had only a few
businesses and professional men, almost all mentioned in Emily's diary.
Luis Cowdry kept the restaurant, Griffin and Hestal (Emily calls him
Hurtel) had the general store, Taylor Green was a lumber dealer and
building contractor, his son William Green was an appraiser, Mrs. Grebe
kept the Beulah Hotel, John D. Waldo was justice of the peace, the Reverend J. B. Self was minister of the Presbyterian Church, W. J. Baltzell
was a painter, Dr. McNelan was the town doctor and pharmacist, and
Jacob Epler sold secondhand goods and real estate. The prominent Elbert
landowners, like the Oaks, Brazeltons, and Greens, owned ranches on
watercourses; the poorer landowners, like Marsena French and his neighbor Purley Foote, homesteaded dryland farms on the high rolling prairie
east of Elbert.*[35]

*The Fricks were the wealthiest Elbert family, and owned most of the
land in town, which they donated to the school and railroad. Jacob and
Mary Frick were Austrian emigrants who in 1866 had built the first
house in Elbert, a double log cabin, and probably the very house Emily
and Annis rented in 1890 from Mary Frick. They shared the double
house with John and Barbara Sloan and their two children, English emigrants of 1887.*[36]

Mary Frick and the Sloans were friends of Emily's, as were the Baltzells and Mrs. Sam Griffin, but her "very best friend" was Maria Ann Oaks, the wife of Joseph Oaks who had developed an 1861 squatter's claim into a 2,000-acre ranch just north of Elbert. The Oaks's two-story house had the only inside plumbing in Elbert.[37]

Tracks of the Denver and Fort Worth Railway (formerly the Denver and New Orleans and the Denver Texas and Gulf) were built in 1882 right through the middle of Elbert. A daily train made the twelve-hour round trip between Denver and Colorado Springs with stops at Elizabeth and Elbert. Emily could not afford to take the train; she drove her buggy to Denver in a day and a half in good weather, stopping for meals and lodging along the way at houses at Elizabeth, Frankstown (now Franktown), and Parker.[38]

The county seat of Elbert County was not Elbert but Kiowa, 10 miles northwest; another community mentioned in the diary was Bijou Basin, at the headwaters of Bijou Creek 6 miles southeast of Elbert, where Charles Mathews and the Killians had ranches.

Jan 1st 1890

Emily L. French   Elbert Colorado.
Let me only in the fear of God put on these pages what shall transpire in my poor life. Pure truths are only of value. I seek not the aplause of the people only that I may deserve the epitaph—She hath done what she could.

January, Wednesday 1, 1890

God be with me through this year.
Had a good night rest—did not waken till I heard Annis making the fire. I fell asleep & did not waken till she came to the door & flung it open, wished me a happy new year. I thanked her, got up & left—Ollie sleeping. We went to see them, the girls of Elbert, at the Dance in the hall last night—staid till 10. Ollie & I went to Mr. Joe Oaks, got 2 sacks of hay & brought home. This morning we both got a large armful of wood & brought in as a mark that we will bring in something the whole year, we so need to. Ollie got breakfast, then we went to cleaning up the house. I have not felt like it since I moved into Mrs. Fricks house. We cleaned the

window, put up little white curtains. The carpet & chairs make it
look home—like Mr Sloans, the family living in the other part.
He fixed a light of glass in my window. He went to Denver
tonight, took a cap to Dannie. His wife expects confinement any
day, hope he will return soon. Made 3 pies, some buiscuits,
cooked some cranberries. Ollie at work on her school dress—
["Letter Register"]: J. E. Jones/Dunn   Jan 1 saw T. *Green*
["Visits"]: Jan 1st Mrs. Sloan came in from other room with her
children, she so near confinement.

January, Thursday 2, 1890

I need the ever hour dear Lord stay though near by. Amen.
Got up early but was so choked up could scarcely breath, eat a
hasty breakfast, left Ollie in bed. I went to Mrs. Baltzells to wash,
she had no wood so I could not. I went then to Mrs. Fricks—I
sewed for a while on Florence's apron, then the last sewing machine needle broke, I sewed by hand, put on some ricrack braid,
made some nuddles for her dinner. She asked me to stay, I
thought not best, came home. Ollie got mother a good dinner, oh
how I do wish I might have her always with me. I fitted her green
dress, got it nice, fitted a pattern for her so she can make her one
for school. We went, she & I, to Mrs. Baltzell to stitch the dress. It
verry cold so I could not speak out loud, my cold so verry tight.
—I went over to Mrs. Fricks to get a rooster. Ollie staid to supper
with Mrs Baltzell. I eat a little with Mrs F, some Blood sausage,
the first I ever eat, not bad. We got home, I so bad. She made a
fire in the fire place, warmed the kettle, made me a hot lemonade.
I went to bed oh so sick, my cold.

January, Friday 3, 1890

I got up determined to go to Mrs Oaks' to wash. I made me some
tea, eat a bite, left Ollie frying some potatoes for her breakfast &
Annis, she knitting on my blue stockings. She tried to get them
done for a Newyears present. I took my little pail to get milk. I
went to work at 8, had my white clothes on the line before dinner. Mrs Maxon came in as we set down, she so gossipy, nothing
weighty to her, she talked for 1 hour, I went on working. Got
done at 3, cleaned the kitchen, Laura helped me. Ollie came in

time to hang up some of the colored clothes. Sewed some on the machine for Mrs. Oaks. I cleaned the water closet, it so *bad*. Earl sits on the floor always. I went at the Ironing, done over half before supper—had fried potatoes, meat, milkgrava, tea & bread. I got the chimese of mine that I had washed here. She gave me a nice lot of dry bread, some milk. I left Ollie to stay with Laura all night—I came home so tired, went straight to my rest thanking god I feel so much better of my cold—

January, Saturday 4, 1890

I must again part with my child, God help us both.

I up early to get Ollie's dress as near finished as possible. She, dear child, must go to her school so as to be there monday morn. I have to live so far separated from my dear children—I try to cheer up, oh why am I so persecuted by the one of all others that should protect me? Bound the waist, put the puffs on the sleeves, worked the button-holes—She came after her dinner, Mrs O kept her. She has had one good treat, she did want to see the girls so much, she mended her red Fascinator, got ready a nice lunch for her & mother so we could eat again together. Laura came, we had to hurry for the train is on time, Mr Sloan says. He is so kind to see to it. He took her satchel down for us or we should have missed, I think. I got a Dunn from Jones Livery at Elizabeth, C Wyght should have paid it, Fannys keeping. He was paid by us. I got a nice Old rooster borrowed of Mrs. Frick. I met Taylor Green. [Added later]: Found a few body lice on Annis, must have come from Myron.

["Visits"]: 4 Laura Oaks came to see *Ollie,* she has fix my front room so nice—put curtains (my table cover cut in two) at the windows, a red cover on the mantle over the fireplace, some old carpet on the floor, *&c.*

January, Sunday 5, 1890

Up before daylight, I must take A to her Ranche, it is quite a while since she was there. They are bound to take it from her if they can—I took some bread, potatoes, rice, meal, sugar, dried apples, onions, Bacon, milk, and 2 quilts, a pair of blankets & a pillow so she can be comfortable. We met Mr Waldo, had a talk with him, he seems to be all right—we have to trust someone. I made a fire, thawed out the kettle & pail so to go to the spring & get her some clean water. I fixed a dummy in the buggy, 'twas well I did. I went on to the spring, he sprung out of the house after me, I never stoped once. When I got up there he sprung on the platform, had a pail, said I could have no water. I told him I should. He commenced his low talk. I told him I came for water, not to see or hear from him. I had a witness that would defend *mother*. He went to drawing but kept up his tyrade, such a string. I told him he ought to be ashamed, he took a young virtuous girl from her fathers house. He said I was as good as I was then. I told him he had just told the truth he never ment to. I took my *rag* child, started home. Annis with her fire & supper most ready now. She all right.

January, Monday 6, 1890
There is a friend that sticketh closer than a brother
Got up early, had my own fire to build, Annis at the ranch, I got it right off for a wonder. I coocked some oatmeal, made a nice cup of tea, mended my apron, combed my hair, got ready to go to Mrs Baltzell to wash. Mr Sloan to feed the horse. Found all the family sick with colds, could not wash today. I went over to Mrs Oaks, she just crawling arround. I cleared her table, made out the bread, washed & cleaned all the forenoon. She gave me squash & milk, meat, bread, & a pan a hole in it. I got a bottle of sulphur & a wash pan in at Mrs. Dobbins Old house, carried all home, eat a lunch. Went over to Mrs Fricks to calcemine, she just getting dinner for Gotleib & her brother. They hauled a load of straw. She made stew, egg fritters, a strong cup of coffee I cannot drink. She did not want to clean today, she cut out a chimmese. I sewed till dark, went over to Baltzells to see if I could get a brush, his wore out. Brought a pail for the horse. Write till late in this and the last year. Sloans made me a cup of tea, *nice*. I carried comfort & Annis's easy chair in to Mrs. Sloan. She has waited her confinement three weeks, is discouraged.

January, Tuesday 7, 1890
I will not fail thee, nor forsake thee Amen
I have a headache this morning but duty calls me, I must go to help Mrs Frick. Oh such a strange dream, so real, I was loved and

engaged to some one, where are they? *They* seemed quite old,
where & when shall such a thing come? I went over, on the way
got my whitewash brush of Mrs. Cowdry. Had a good long talk
with Grandma Kenedy, she is getting so old, helps them in their
eating house. I went on over to Mrs. Fricks, she washing. I
cleared the room, ready to go to calcomining. It is three colors,
Blue, yellow & smoke. I sewed till noon, she made a soup. I gave
Eugene & his Uncle Joseph Cook a card, they hauled a load of
straw. She went out to jabber to them, I went on alone calcimin-
ing. She came in, went to work stopping the holes with paste &
cloth. I was till after dark cleaning, then we had mush & a little
milk. I helped wash the dishes. She said I must stay all night. I sat
by the fire, it so cold. I wish I was with my children so often—
how I suffer, shall anyone ever know? I went up stairs to bed.
They sleep all together down in the hall I have just cleaned. How
they *enjoy*.

January, Wednesday 8, 1890
Who is a God like unto thee pardoning all
I up at the Fricks at 6, came home—made a fire, got my breakfast. Mrs Sloan not so well. I went to Baltzells to wash. It is cold.
She had the water on, so I shall be allowed to wash. Oh such
work, and such a lot of dirty & old clothes not scarcely fit to
wash, she not able to buy others. I got them ready for the line, the
wind so hard, yet I managed to hang all out. The tub frozen full
of water, I worked at 2 hours before I could get enough of it out
so I could put the clothes in. I washed an Old coat, then cleaned
up so to Iron. She had roast pork with dressing, homminy, buiscuits & butter, coffee. I was tired but enjoyed my supper much.
Went at the Ironing. The girls broke a plate fooling. I done all the
clothes, was dry. She paid me, gave me some food to carry home.
I wore an old coat, cold. [Later]: I came home, Mrs. Sloan had
been some sick all day. I lay down, told them to call me at 1.
They did, I sent out for Dr Higgins.

January, Thursday 9, 1890
He will be our god even unto the end
I went to wash for Mrs. Oaks today. I am not able to work a sin-

gle minute, yet here I am & must do the work, well or sick.
Mrs. Sloans sick all the night, I up with her, the child a girl, still
born at 8 this morning. She has a strange growth in her abdomen.
Her Annie, 16 months old, is her baby yet. I put all away as best I
could, got a place for the child, a nice smooth box. I had made her
as comfortable as we could, the Dr promising to come in the
morning. I lay down at 4 but did not rest much. I am in no shape
to work. I darkened her windows, then on to my work. I cleared
Mrs Oaks table as usual, then after waiting for the clothes & putting the water over, got at the washing. Such dirty clothes, I cannot seem to get them clean. Laura is so bad with her clothes, I will
have to scald both dresses & aprons sure. Agnes came with the
toothache, she wanted to have it out. She was going, met Mother
Clibon, she said dont, so the poor girl will go home & wait. I
cleaned the floor, ironed some.

January, Friday 10, 1890

He that believeth on the son hath everlasting life? Lord I believe—
I am so tired this morning. I did not hurry to get started, just took
my time which I ought always to do. I eat my breakfast alone,
then picked up the clothes from Mrs Sloans & my own. He put
on the boiler, I got her clothes through two waters, then they
were so I could put them in to wash. Such clothes are always hard
to wash. I have a large lot for us both, 2 quilt for me, 1 for her,
flannels &c. I done all by 4, then I cleaned my old chairs, my
dishes &c, then my floor which was so verry dirty I scrubbed and
rinsed. Then I went by Mrs Sloans fire to warm, the first I have
been by today. I am so troubled about my wood, yet I have
hauled wood & coal that French has warmed by this winter thus
far. I put on my new stockings after warming my feet in warm
water. The pup R. draged & tore the clothes.

January, Saturday 11, 1890

I got up after a restless night, eat a cold lunch, did not make a fire.
I must go to pick up chips that Mrs. Dobbins left on her yard. I
took 4 sack & any straw tick to fill at Mrs Fricks. I filled my sacks
& a barrel and a box with chips. A Kerosene can was in the barrel.
Mrs Oaks came over, said she would take it, then return it. I had

to go empty my chips, then fill up the barrel again. Then went to fill my straw tick, Florence helped me with it. They have a lot of young pigeons in the barn. I saw a hen sick, told her how to put kerosene on its head for lice. She caught it, I turned my shawl, it all straw. Went back. Mr Sloan caught his horse, Dick got him ready. I got Jamesie dressed, he so troublesome & his mother in bed. I went back on foot, helped load the tick, tied it on, then after the chips. It snowing hard. Got back with some milk & F. made a break for the pasture. Then I warmed, started for Annis. She all right. I fixed the house, salted the horses, came back. A train on track, Dick came near getting us upset sure.

January, Sunday 12, 1890

Help thou my unbelief—Amen

The day of rest, to sinfull mortals given, help me my dear heavenly father to keep this day to thyself. I arose at 7, got our breakfast—Annis so cold, cannot seem to get herself warm. She wrote a letter to Lee Ramsey sending him back the check for what he has, that he make it on the German National Bank instead. He has always treated her so fairly, few if any have so much manliness. I went in and made Mrs Sloans bed, washed & combed the children and swept the floor. Jamesie is a bad child, will not mind one word is said to him. I came in our room, washed sister, she was fearful black after being 1 week at the ranche. She saw Old French kill chicken, empty vessels, and things he never thought of doing when I was with him. He tried Annis door twice after dark—I made us a good cup of tea, we eat some squash pie, sat by the fire, so cozy. Old Mr Burris he died Friday night, was buried this afternoon.

January, Monday 13, 1890

He that has the true measure of faith God strengthens

Annis up 7, had me a nice fire but did not put anything on for breakfast, I cooked some oatmeal and we had the old Soup, glad of that. Think of it, we girls ought to have a thousand dollars each today and he is even trying to get her ranche away from her. I should not be here tonight writing this by the dim light of a candle only for his base treachery. Thank God I have my two children, if only my health does not fail me. I work to hard, they all

say I have always done that. He was so lazy I had to, but I am trying to be more careful of myself, I must—I done Mrs Sloans ironing and carried it in to her, got my rocking chair and a quilt and
Annis soap stone. Got her up and made her bed. She sat up 2
hours, seemed to feel all right. I swept her floor 3 times today,
made yeast and fixed the bread, made her a mess of buiscuits & at
noon a mess of griddle cakes. I got all ready to put on a rug for
Mrs F but it got to late so I will try to get it on in the morning. I
must do all I can to pay my rent. Annis is ripping old Frenches
piss stained breeches only to see them, the old whiskey bloat.

January, Tuesday 14, 1890

The true measure of faith for us oh Lord

I coughed & shivered all night. Arose at 7, Annis had a fire & my
oatmeal cooked. I nearly froze getting the *rest.* It is one of the
coldest days. She combed my *hair.* The stove smoked so we had
to go in at the fire place and let the fire in the stove go out. I took
down the stove pipe and cleaned the soot out, so if it would burn
it could, but no use, it drew into the kitchen. I went into Mrs
Sloan's and mixed her bread. She did not have enough flour so I
took the graham flour I had to finish it out. She gave me a loaf of
the bread, I coocked her some apples, made her a cup of tea. She
gave me some. I took it in, gave Annis some. I sewed the rug on
the frames and put a piece of Brussels carpet in the center. It will
save a lot of reaching and be more durable. Mr Sloan joked me
and no wonder, I was all covered with soot—on my neck. I came
where I could see in the glass, then I got some warm water &
soap. He came into our room after he had fed the horse—never
saw anyone work a rug before, tis hard work. How bitter cold it
is tonight—

January, Wednesday 15, 1890

According to your faith be it unto you—

Shall we freeze to death? that is the serious question with us now.
18 below zero this morning & growing colder. I wakened with
one of my feet so cold and the frost on the covers. So much for
Elbert, Colo. I warmed my breakfast as best I could, combed my
hair, got off to wash at Mrs Baltzells, she trying to get Alice off
for her school. It so cold she would not wash till next week. I am

not sorry. I was given a nice dish of vegetable soup, I brought it home to Mrs. Sloan. She sat up about 3 hours. I put a new front in Annie's apron, done a lot on the rug. I am writing this tonight by the light of the fire place. I picked up coal & wood today. The sparks are all comeing in clouds, can it be I am to have money, like hints that god can & will help me & that very soon. I seem to have just that—faith. I must have a little supper, then go to my rest. my *children*

January, Thursday 16, 1890
When he had spoken he showed his hands & feet
I coughed so all night—I felt to weak to get up. I got my tea & started off to wash for Mrs Oaks. She always is so good to me. I feel like I could do more when I am treated well. She had a big wash, 7 sheets, 5 pairs pillow slips, 6 white aprons. I had them ready to hang up at noon, but Charley wanted his reader covered so I stopped and covered it. Carrie Shimpf staid all night with Laura & came back at noon. It took all the noon to get them fed & back to school. Then Mrs Ewen came. Mrs Oaks was at work baking a cake for his birthday. He stoped on his way from the ranche, was going out to the mill at Brazeltons to get a load of sawdust so to put up their own ice, said he wanted her to go out to the ranche. Friday they would kill the hogs, they have some big fat ones—I got done 4, then cleaned the floor, put some carpet by the table for Laura to stand on to wash the dishes. I finished the floor, filled the reservoir, helped her get some potatoes on, went & sat down while she finished the supper, I was so tired. Mrs. Ewen going to Oregon, this her good bye visit. All down on Mrs King.
["Letter Register"]: Jan 16th a letter from Olive, Daniel & Mrs. Larkins. Does ever fate fall on a person surely it is following them, he sick all the time, Dannie is, with a cold, but some better. I wrote right back to them, I will not let them wait as I have been made to so much.

January, Friday 17, 1890
Now we see through a glass darkly! then face to face
I so near sick I did not hurry to get started this morning. I got a nice letter from Olive & Daniel, I answered it. She is elected this

week editress of their school paper. She wanted mother to help
her some, so I wrote a little to put in. Told her how I used to *manage*. This experience will be a help to her. She says Daniel is doing
well, thank a good God. How I pray as well as work for their ad-
vancement. I do trust my dear heavenly father all will yet come
out right. I got 25 cts Oatmeal, 10 c. envelopes, 5 c. postage, sent
her a letter. I direct it in care of Addie Quick 234 Thurman St.
Jerome Park. That is a blind—I do not intend they shall find my
children. I changed Mrs. Sloan's tick, a sheep's wool she was sick
on, into an old one of mine so I could wash it. I got my clothes on
the line. It broke and they all went into the dirt. I never lost my
temper but took them up, put them into the tub, finished as best I
could, and got my own supper. She is up again, doing what she
can for herself, baked nice bread, gave us a loaf. Annis is at work
on the rug. She tries to help me, poor girl. How the stove does
smoke almost all the time, no let up.

January, Saturday 18, 1890

> *It is written: Eye hath not seen nor ear heard*

I waited till I had breakfast, then I went in to Mrs. Sloan's to finish
putting up the clothes that fell in the dirt yesterday. He staid from
his wood cutting at the schoolhouse. It was a big job and the wind
so hard. He is buying of Ewens a span of horses & a beadsted,
some water barrels &c. He brought home an old saddle, she
laughed, said they would all starve in this country. She is about
right—not much money here that is sure. I got the clothes on the
line. While I was hanging them up, saw the funeral of Ralph
Chapman go by. He died at Colorado Springs, his widowed
mother had him brought here and laid beside his father. She has 5
left, 3 sons, 2 daughters. Taylor Green spoke the few words at the
funeral. They took the corpse from the train to the church last
night. Had I been not so buisy I should have known of it and
gone. It is as well I guess—I cleaned Mrs S floor, she had beef &
dumplings for dinner, I eat with her. Laura Oaks, Charley &
George came in to tell me about the funeral. I let Laura read
Olive's letter to her mother—

["Visits"]: 18 Laura, Charley & George Oaks came to see us, I
showed her Ollies letter, she is so good, thank the lord I have a
few friends.

January, Sunday 19, 1890

Shall I & my dear *children be of his* chosen

How I do long to be near my children. God only knows the real desire of my heart. How unhappy I realy am, will he bring me a home? he can. I trust him in all things. I can truly say thy will be done, yet it is only human to be a little impatient. I got up, dressed in my black dress, took my good old horse Ric her Oats. She waits at the gate for them. Then I went on to Mrs Oaks to get some milk. Laura, eating her breakfast pancakes & coffee, asked me to join her, so I did. The boys all looking over to see the Sunday mooveing of the Depot onto the other side of the track. At 9 they had it across, seems a host of men all at work to get it into its new place. I was surprised at it. I helped Laura as I do her mother. She gave me some meat & bread, some milk. I swept up the front room & the kitchen, came home. Annis had burned up the bread I put on to steam. She seems to forget so easy. She combed my hair, washed my neck. I made a fire in the fireplace. How I do wish I could have a nice cheerful companion to sit opposite me.

January, Monday 20, 1890

Better it is to be of an humble spirit with the lowly than to divide the spoil with the proud

I feel so homesick this morning—hearing Mrs. Sloan singing it just makes me think of the home away in Iowa, where if I *ever* had any happy days, I tried to be happy. I have always worked hard, too hard. My bent shoulders, my crippled hard hands all go to show I have never rested when there was any work to be done. This morning I go about trying to clean up the few dishes we have, and putting everything to rights. Annis got angry because I wanted her to wash & comb. How dirty she sits day after day. I got the water & soap & just forced her to clean up. The stove smokes near all the time, we can scarce cook a meal. I made an onion stew on Mrs Sloan's stove, and put some of the dry bread in that is given to me where I work. I mended Dan's saddle horn and put the holdback strap back on my harness. I worked on my pillow shams, "Good morning" and "Good Night". Mrs. Sloan invited us in there to sit by her light & fire, *nice*. We spent Sunday evening in Mrs Sloan's, had a nice chat. I had been wishing for something of the kind, she invited us.

January, Tuesday 21, 1890

I dreamed a pleasant life for myself and *children,* only to wake and find the same starring me in the face—I got oatmeal & tea that was left of the tea Mrs Sloan made for us last night. So kind of her. I scoured knives, forks, and spoons, what for I cannot see. No one will come to see us, that is sure. I got ready to go to wash for Mrs Baltzell. I got there, *no water.* She thought we could not wash. I told her I could bring it from the creek near. She concluded I might go on with it. I brought a boiler full, & after he had his breakfast he hitched up Snort to his buckboard and got 2 tubs full, then we was all right. A large washing, she waits 2 weeks. I have made up my mind to have him paint my buggy & I wash for her for it, then she will have it done every week. It is so hard when it runs 2 weeks. She says she will do so. I know not how we shall get enough to eat but God has always helped me, he will now. I am trusting and working day by day. I put on another rug for Annis to work at. She is doing well—

January, Wednesday 22, 1890

Mrs Baltzell lent me a lamp after I had done the washing & ironing

January, Thursday 23, 1890

Went this morning before 7 to get a lamp chimney. Must wash for Mrs. Oaks, I am not well. Mrs. John Ewen was there with 2 of the children—

January, Friday 24, 1890

Carried the drugs I had to Dr Higgins, got some carbolic acid to Dr, Old Ric her back is so sore.

January, Saturday 25, 1890

Up early as I must accomplish much today. Got a nice roast at the new butcher shop kept by Salleen, the kid. Mr Sloan brought from the Post-office a large letter which proved to be the will I had Judge Liddell to add a codocil in his name. I shall get some one to witness and return. John Sloan, Mary Frick.

["Letter Register"]: Jan 25 a letter from Liddell, he is true, witnessed the paper & sent it back. Tuesday a letter, Dan sick.

January, Sunday 26, 1890

> Had Mr & Mrs Sloan to dinner
>
> ["Letter Register"]: I got dinner for Mr & Mrs Sloan, James &
> Anna their children. While we were at table Mrs. Frick came. I
> had her sit down with, afterwards had her & Mr Sloan witness the
> codicil of my will.

January, Monday 27, 1890

> Moved them with a high wind.

January, Tuesday 28, 1890

> Came home from Mrs Sloans, got a big load of wood, saw Mrs
> Dell Geargia and her little girl Gracie, she going into the house
> where Jack Baldwin lives. He has married Hattie Moore, Dannie's
> teacher in the Elbert school.

January, Wednesday 29, 1890

> Washed all day at Mrs Baltzells, cleaned the floor, ironed some.
> Laura Oaks took a music lesson of him. She would learn if only
> there was order in the home. She lives in such a home, the boys
> cursing.

January, Thursday 30, 1890

> Washed all day a big lot clothes for Mrs Oaks. She gave me cof-
> fee, cake, a loaf of bread, some milk.

January, Friday 31, 1890

> Fixed Balze Gaylors vest—helped Mrs Oaks, she is almost down.
> She had the boys get a horse to take her to the candy pulling at the
> "Beulah" hotel kept by Mrs Grebe.

February, Saturday 1, 1890

> Took Ric to the ranche, got some wood. Got a letter from Olive,
> Dannie is sick, she wrote on the 27th, the letter went to Omaha,
> Cook Co, Neb., missent.

February, Sunday 2, 1890

> Am going to start for Denver with Fanny, she is so slow—she

took the Frankstown road as though that was the route I must follow. Old Pap Mellor on the watch, the scamps they all want to
steal all they can from this poor girl. I got as far as Rowley's, staid
all night, they always treat me as if I was good enough for an associate.

["Letter Register"]: Feb 2, started to drive to Denver, went the
road to Franktown, old man Mellor saw me. The verry devil is
helping them.

February, Monday 3, 1890

I got as far as Mr Rowleys last night. It was real dark, the moon
came up. He went to Denver yesterday. This morning I got an
early start—I must get through as soon as I can. I drove all the
way, 24 miles, got there at 1 oclock. They had given me up, did
not look for me any more. I went down to see Liddell, he did not
expect me. I got $15.00 to pay my grocery bill and get the buggy
fixed, it needs repairs.

February, Tuesday 4, 1890

I took the first rest for over 1 week, needed it so much. Olive
wanted her hair cut, so I took her to the Medina hair store. Had to
pay 50 c. to get it done. I left her to go back in the P.M. I went to
L. A. Melborn wagon shop, got the front bound, a new whip
socket, a cover to the back of the seat, leathers on the tugs. Went
to the Depot for Mrs Oaks, she though she could come down
this week sure. Not there, something out of the way. Mrs.
Larkins went with me to the city. I got a pie and some fried cake
for a lunch, we had to stand. Mrs. Howell gave me some red flannel to put on Dannies throat, he seems to be so hoarse all the
time.

February, Wednesday 5, 1890

Dannie a good deal better so he could go to school today. His
throat begins to get sore out-side, he breathes better. I must clean
the kitchen, it is so verry dirty. Mrs Larkins is not well and he is
just skin and bones. Mrs. Howell gave me some flannel for his
throat and a gargle, so good of her. Could I stay home with the
children I could have them so comfortable. I cut his pants out,

will try to get them made so he will not get so raged. I mended
his clothes, his socks, everything I could find. They wait for
mother to come home, all of them, even Luella—Agnes seems so
glad when I am at home, the little dear. She is a good child.

February, Thursday 6, 1890

It is raining to day, I cannot go home to Elbert. Will repair for the
children, get some wood &c, and be ready to start in the morning. I cut my calico dress, black striped. I gave Mrs. L. one like it,
she has hers most worn out. They got dinner for me. I could not
eat breakfast with the children. Olive is so cross in the morning.
Beef, oatmeal, canned pears, tea, bread—all so nice. They always
do something to make me feel as if I had a home. I might have
found a worse lot of folks to deal with. They are temperate, virtuous & so honest, I leave my things unlocked and never a thing is
disturbed—

February, Friday 7, 1890

We up early, everything going nice. Olive sees it will never do the
way she is managing, she must be kind. We got the work all
done. I started at school time as they did. All of us are in good
humor. Mr Larkins would like to go home with me, if it was not
so cold I would urge it. I drove after Mr Corbin's dairy wagon up
on Colfax ave, water at the bridge. Got a lunch and farther on a
spool of black thread. I stoped at the 12 mile house to feed Fanny,
fed in an old cart. Got a poor lunch made by my own tea—an old
maid kept rattling on, she is not bright. Melvin's are their names.
I went on, got to Mrs. Rowleys at 5. Maggie was alone, she asked
me to get out. I helped her to start the fire. Mrs. Rowley came, a
Mrs Bonny with her, a neighbor. I mended my sack & vail—I
slept with her, he being away. I did not rest verry much, I was
afraid I would snore and disturb her—

February, Saturday 8, 1890

I started at 9 after a good warm breakfast—fried potatoes, buiscuit, tomato preserves, meat-cream gravy, tea, so good. I bid
them good morning—Fanny goes so slow I could walk almost as
fast, but I must always be draging around. I met Mr Rowley, he

had come with a friend, sent home a new lumber wagon. They
are such nice, stirring people. He joked me, said he always liked
to have the goodlooking widows come along. I stoped at a Mrs.
Allisons, got a Plymouth Rock Rooster 40¢ he is young. They put
him in a sack. I had a box so he rode all right. I stoped at a stone
house, a Mrs Campbell's, for dinner and to feed my horse. I had
meat, bread, tea, grape jelly, good. An old man so crippled up,
she said he had always been an old crank, never worked much. Be
sure our sin will find us out. I went in through the ranche, left a
lot, got the buggy seat—

["Letter Register"]: I came back Sat 8th, found Elmer Colman had
come here with Taylor Green, scared her, Annis, into selling him
the horse or mare Doll.

February, Sunday 9, 1890

Annis played hob while I was gone. I never thought Taylor Green
would do a mean thing for pay. He came here with Elmer Colman, they together come and intimidated Annis to paying a debt
of $15.00 that French owed to Griffin and Hurtel, a nice job for
them surely. What is the girl to do, she has not mind enough to
see into anything, and they come when I am gone—I put the coal
into sacks, also some wood, her commode, and drove over, put
them in the house, went and looked for the colts, saw them sure.
Rock is growing, so is Roxy, she has a white stripe in the face.
The gray colt is large enough to drive. I went to Mr. Waldo's, got
the buggy tongue, had Ric to lead. Came home, met Oaks &
French, loaded the buggy all ready to haul a few things to Denver.
I am not going to stay here much longer. I met French with Joe
Oaks. Dr Higgins is away in Denver, I saw him Wednesday eve,
so old soapsuds goes.

["Letter Register"]: I went to the ranch Sunday the 9th, got Ric,
the pole & put the 2 chairs, feather bed, home made stand in, got
ready to start for Denver.

February, Monday 10, 1890

Up at 1 A.M., fed the horses grain & hay, caught the chickens and
tied them so they can be safe in the basket & box, had my breakfast at 3, oatmeal & tea, started at 4½. On the way tried to hitch

Ric beside Fanny, no go. She will not lead good. I had 1 stand, 2 chairs, 1 rocker, my feather bed, a few tins, the chopping bowl. I turned into the road leading out by the sheep ranch, 2 of the chickens got away. Was going along, the sun shining so nice, suddenly it grew dark, the wind blew oh so hard. Mrs. Fear put 2 warm Irons in the bed, she never said a thing but showed me to rest, I found them, could hug *her*.

["Letter Register"]: Mon the 10th, went by the way of Elizabeth, got caught in that awful storm, a man perished 3 miles out on the way to his home, Denver. God saved poor me. I went into the old Reynolds house, I had been there before, knew where I was. His sister and her husband & the father Farr did what they could to thaw me out.

February, Tuesday 11, 1890

We not up till 9 oclock, it cold and stormy, they said I could not go. The chickens down cellar—Mrs Far a thick set woman 25, just my style of woman. I made a pair of mittens and we sewed on a gown for Mrs Johnson, had mush & milk. Old Mr Far not able to be about, lies on the bed most of the time, said he wished he was able to hire a nurse.

["Letter Register"]: I stayed Tuesday 11th . . .

February, Wednesday 12, 1890

I up early to get a start, she got ahead of me in building the fire. I had to stop at Woodburys to get the buggy greased.

["Letter Register"]: Started 12th, the roads bad drifted, I was till dark on my way, got there, the 2 horses tired. I went to Reddingtons, got a pail of hay, a sack of oats so I can feed a few days.

February, Thursday 13, 1890

Early up, Olive had potatoes & meat, nice bread. Mrs L. made me some tea. Mr L going with me to get a new double harness, we went to the Denver Harness Manufactory 17th & Holiday, got the Halters repaired & strap to the neckyoke all for $25.50. I gave him 25¢ to get him a lunch, then I went to Liddell to get $10.00 so I can get a good harness. I got a 15¢ dinner, such a rowdy place. I had them fixing the buggy tongue on 19 st, $1.50, put straps on.

February, Friday 14, 1890

Early start, Olive got breakfast, we eat. Then she thought she has to wash collars so I let her stay ½ day home. We, Mrs Larkins, Agnes, & Daniel, took the new harness pole & buggy, went to Mr & Mrs Nickolas out by the Gentlemans Driving Park—at the Clifton house on Larimer, 225, Mrs. N told me I could get a puppy. Olive and Daniel invited to a Valentine Party at Mr Everets. Mr Quick here to make trouble.

February, Saturday 15, 1890

A late start. I must go with Olive to get her hair frized, and if they have brought the dogs I will get a collar & chain. I got them, took them to the house I live in when I can, near the bridge below the Larimer St Bridge & Viaduct & nearly oposite Corbins dairy. The dogs all got loose & run home, no use to try unless we take a pup and raise it—Started at noon, Mr Larkins went with me to the river to water the horses. Daniel runs all over, Olive out hunting him. Oh dear, will he ever see in Olive & mother friends that he must help instead of bother. I drove on thinking oh such hard thoughts—why is this life for me, a *home lover*? I do so crave a *home,* will I ever have a *home*? I got as far as Mrs Woodburys tonight. It is so cold. Girls hand better.

February, Sunday 16, 1890

On the way after such a plain breakfast, only fried potatoes & bread & tea. I helped wash the dishes, got the clothes off the line that the girl they have to help them, I slept with her last night, she seems to be a real nice quiet person. The hired man got the horses, hitched on my buggy, greased. I bid them good morning—went on, it cold. I decided to go as I went, by the Elizabeth route, as Mary Rowley did not come with me. Mr & Mrs Far came out of their gate after I passed and I saw their wonderful dog & knew it to be them, so I waited.

February, Monday 17, 1890

Got up at Mrs. Brooks, she so poorly. I done all that I could to help her, swept the whole house, cleared and washed the breakfast dishes. He watered and hitched up Fanny and Ric. At 9 I started,

the wind always is tearing around this terrible Colorado. I drove
straight towards home, inquired on the way for the right road to
Denver. I had a fearful time going down the roads fenced up. On
the road that goes out from the Merino sheep farm I did not know
it, so I had a bad drive. Led old Fanny—Ric hitched behind,
down I go into a gully. Got to my poor home 2 P.M., Annis hard
at work on the buggy rug. She does at times seem to try. What
can I do, must I go on liveing this way, no use to try to make a
companion of her, she is so *dull*. Eat supper at Mrs Baltzells, she
glad to see. Blackberries, bread, tea, I brought a basinfull home.

February, Tuesday 18, 1890

I wrote a letter to the Historical Pub Co., 1 to the Ladies journal,
1 to Will Foote, he came in the P.M. I had gone to Mrs Baltzells
to fit my striped black & white calico dress. She left the children
with me, went to see Mrs Oaks. She verry low, cannot live many
days. Laura does not seem to care, the others all show it. I shall
not let Olive see her any more than I can avoid. L is bad. Mr
Sloan here today, he is real lame. I took a load of coal & wood to
the ranche, got the doll cradle & Hamiltons shoes to let Mrs Sloan
have them. I took the buggy over to Mr Baltzells for him to begin
painting it. That is the way I have agreed to take my pay. Fanny,
after I had her unhitched, threw up her head, caught the bridle,
broke it. She always does that. I had Fanny, went over the high
bluffs, came across a three wire fence & 2 gates. I got a little hay
at Mr Oaks, Willie Green there. She at Deaths door, a good
woman, my verry best friend.

February, Wednesday 19, 1890

I had got my breakfast & moved the rug for Annis, then gone to
Mrs Baltzells to see if she would not wash tomorrow. It is so long
since I washed for her, so much has happened, how can I wait
here in this burg. I met Laura as she came from Miss Raibley to
get her to wash. I told her I was ready to work for them when
they wanted me. She acts funny but I care not. It was just dark, I
was in the buggy with old Fanny, she is tired and thin.

February, Thursday 20, 1890

I am not verry well but am going to wash for Mrs. Baltzell today.

She is kind and considerate of my feelings, that is worth a great deal to me. A big washing, a good dinner—pork & beans, cabbage—he such a pleasant man in his family. It does make me feel so bad when I think how hard I have tried to make a good home. Now I will only seem to be what I am not, contented.

February, Friday 21, 1890

I got my breakfast, then took my dress over to Mrs. Baltzells to fit it. Mr Baltzell so lame this morning, she will take the horse and hitch for him. I let him take Roxey today. We have no feed, he is feeding for us. Today is mail day, he carries it to Bijou Basin. I washed off the buggy wheels and running gear so he can finish painting. He began it yesterday so I am sure to get it done before I must go back to Denver. While we were putting the horse on the buckboard, we saw a black cloth hung out of Mr Oaks front door. *she is dead* oh such a lot of *bad bad* boys left to go to the bad. He has more than most of men on his hands. Mr. Waldo came & told Annis he was going to move her house on her ground tomorrow, so we must be there sure. I want to go to the funeral, so we must work all night to get ready. I scrubbed her all through. All ready at 6 to start.

February, Saturday 22, 1890

Went over at 6 oclock to see if we could take Mr Baltzells buckboard, my buggy he has got detach, wheels off, &c, is painting. Yes, I got it, must hurry back. We watched the sun rise for a fact, so cold I had her bundled good. We was at Mr Waldos before anyone else. We went on & changed Fanny for Ric. I so cold. We started for her ranche, old French blowing around. He is an awful mean old fellow. I never knew he was so till now. I used to think even he was good. I tried to get some potatoes. I had to go & get them, Pearl Foote there but as mean as the old man. Annis got so I had to bring her back, she cant stand much. I asked old French too give the men a lunch. I fed Ric, started at 1 to go back to Elbert. If we can, we will go to Mrs Oaks funeral in time, but Taylor Greene the old Hipocrit, he the only one to talk over her. We went home. Mrs. Frick came, got crackers. I took the buckboard home, he wanted it. They lead Ric & came home. Got a good supper. I got in the mail the story of man book.

February, Sunday 23, 1890

> Up early, caught Ric over too Mrs Fricks. Eat breakfast, then Florence & Eugene going with me to the ranche to set up the stove. We had such a time, I climb on the roof, the wind ripped my skirt off me. I got the stove pipe up there, Florence helped up & down, they both done all they could.

February, Monday 24, 1890

> Went to see C. Mathews if he would come survey Annis land. He passed the house just as we got home, we had a buggy of old wood. I went & talked with him, he would stop all night in town, go in the morning.

February, Tuesday 25, 1890

> I up early, went down as far as Mrs. Griffins to wait for him, eat breakfast there with her. I had lunch. For their dinner she gave me milk in a big bottle. I not wrapped up as I ought to bee, the wind so cold I nearly froze. I drove his surveyors C. Mathews young mare team, they wild. Got to Annis house 4 ocl—so cold I shook.

February, Wednesday 26, 1890

> I up but so sick I could not eat. John Clibon came to see if I could go to wash at his father in-laws for them all. I promised if I should be able. I took the rug in the big basket, went over to Mrs F. I had a chill, in about 1 hour I had to lie down. Joe Isenberg came while I was there, he stayed that night. I slept on the lounge. I coughed so hard she fixed me some ginger tea, done all she could. I took red pepper tea, worked on her rug, cut the scallops all ready to sew.

February, Thursday 27, 1890

> Got up, build both of Mrs Fricks fires. The children came out, Florence helped me start the breakfast—coffee & meat & pancakes. Old Isenberg is lazy, not up till it was on the table. He dont amount to nothing, sets & talks German. I sat on my under teeth, heard them break as I sat down to grind her coffee. Oh dear if only I could get through & go away from all this awful life. God in his mercy do help me, I am so sick, not able to wash for Agnes

& I had said I would. I took a lot of pepper tea, washed the dishes, sat by the fire and worked on the rug. I must get it done if I can today sure, Mrs. F. tries to be kind. She got a good dinner—eggs, coffee & meat, crackers &c. Hellgate came, staid all night. Mrs. Baltzell came to see why I did not go to wash for Agnes, I to sick. I went over to see Agnes in the cold, told her I would try to wash tomorrow if she & John would help me.

February, Friday 28, 1890

I up but oh so sick, coughed an hour. Mrs Frick trying to get breakfast, I done all I was able to help. Isenberg still there. I could not eat anything so I put on my things to go. Mrs Frick said I ought not do such work. I washed at Joseph Oaks, the big days work. Agnes & John helped me good, I could not have done it if they had not. 2 ticks, a quilt, the stained clothes, all that a death can cause. I washed all day, so tired & cold. Laura & Jim went over to Mrs Reeds, not a good place for them. I put on Mrs Oaks cloak, came home. So cold & tired, Annis had a fireplace all nice for me. I sat down a little while, but I had to go to bed. Old Ric I fed good, she so thin. Mr Oaks brought feed, now she will get all she can eat.

March, Saturday 1, 1890

A still day, awful sick all day. Oh dear what shall I do, Old Ric she will have to go hungry, I am not able to feed her.

March, Sunday 2, 1890

I lay still for fear of having a coughing spell. I am so sick & sore, Annis sleeping so sound, she is a carless *nobody*. Oh why am I left with only her for a companion. I called her, then had a hard coughing spell. She made a fire in the grate or fireplace, it smokes so in the stove. She got her own breakfast. The wind not blowing for a wonder. I called old Ric & gave her a feed of oats. She looks so much better, the sore on her back nearly healed, has one now on her neck. I crawled to bed, oh dear I am so sick, wont some-body come, I fear not. My feet are cold. Oh why cannot I have some care when I always have done all in my power for others, must I suffer here alone & make no *sign*. God send me relief.

March, Monday 3, 1890

I felt verry bad when I awoke. Annis crawled out, made a fire, got a little to eat. I lay still, had a hard coughing spell. What will I do, no rest, I am so sore, my kidneys are so weak, I must go see the Dr. Higgins, maybe he will do something to relieve me. I had a fire in the fireplace, it smokes so in the kitchen. I tried to sew, cannot do anything. I am perfectly miserable, what shall I do. Does a kind providence send this terrible affliction for my good, or am I to do something that now I cannot seem to see or understand. My good old faithful horse Ric she must have some hay.

March, Tuesday 4, 1890

I got up and started down to see Dr Higgins, I must do something for this cough. I saw *her,* he in Denver, will be back this morning. I come home, a cat followed me. I took a bottle back to Mrs Griffins, she gave me milk and made me a cup of coffee. She would have me eat a little, she gave me of the cough medicine. I came home, got the letter ready to send a statement, also a check for $3.00 to the His Co. I am going to try to sell a few of their books. I registered a letter, got the receipt, came home, lugged some wood, brought a bag of salt. I so near played out, I will get me too bed. I may rest some, I do not cough so bad as I did at Mrs Griffins. The cough medicine has helped me, she is a good samaritan & she has had lots of troubles. *Mrs Hall*

March, Wednesday 5, 1890

I could not do anything but cough, I eat a little oatmeal, got a sack all ready to put on another rug. We can use the nice rags up this way & have the good of them. Annis tries to do as well as she can. I got it all ready. Mrs. B. came, brought rice & bread so we won't starve. She said I might wash just a few pieces when I was able, when will that be. I gave her some Magazines & books & cards for the children, she went off feeling so good. She read my paper of Divorce & recommends she thought I had some cause to rejoice. If I can only get over this awful cold. I put the rug on the frames so Annis could do some before the week is gone.

March, Thursday 6, 1890

Laura came to see if I was able to wash, no I could not. She said

Agnes would do a few for the baby. She brought in some wood,
then went to school. I wrote to Olive a good letter. I cannot see
what the children mean not to write to me after I do suffer so for
a word from them, can they be all right. Laura came at evening,
brought a warm loaf of bread, a can of milk, some cooked meat, I
am so thankful. I wrote a line to the Historical Pub Co. 810 Olive
St. St. Louis Mo. I am decided to go to work with them selling
books. I must do something to earn my liveing, that old rascal has
robbed us both of nearly all, and I am in such poor health. Can
not I make a liveing at this, etc. I will try it faithfully and god will
help if I have the true spirit.

March, Friday 7, 1890

I get up feeling better than I have for 1 week. I shall have to go see
what I can for Mrs. Baltzell, she is too sew on Dannie's pants. I
went, worked some, done the dishes, cleaned the chamber. She is
looking for Mrs. Chapman & her children, they are going to
move back. I stayed all night, so cold, Laura is a good bedfellow.

March, Saturday 8, 1890

We both not well, got a little breakfast. We put Old Snort on the
buckboard, hauled some water, washed the *didas* [diapers]. Then I
cleaned the floor so nice, but I so tired.

March, Sunday 9, 1890

Got up, had a good break—then cleaned up to go to hear a sermon by Rev Self. He is a well meaning man if he is a Presbeteri-
an. I got old Ric hitched in the new painted buggy, the first that is
good to go church, hope to go many more times with it. The
Text Math 22 to 27 verse, to love the lord with all our powers of
mind & heart, our neighbors as ourselves, I try god knows, he is
our Judge. We came back, I put some potatoes to cook on the fireplace, then I started to go to Mr Hoyts to get them to go & move
Annis closet & henhouse. The wind blew oh so hard. I got there,
they said funny things as I rapped, at the thought was the children
go in the keyhole &c. I went in, they were ashamed. I staid all
night. She will come if he can on Thursday sure, she made me a
bed in the back room, 5 big bedbugs on my pillow, morning had
fried mush.

March, Monday 10, 1890

> I started, it snowing hard. Willis Whitney & wife come just as I started. I picked up a big load of wood, all the buggy would hold. I went back to Maxons house, came out by the church, met Old Joe Oaks, told him I must have some feed again. He said he would see to it, wanted me to wash. I carried my two sets of teeth to the express office, sent to Dr. Drury to mend. I have such luck with under teeth, I dont see what I will do with them.

March, Tuesday 11, 1890

> I got up, could not eat, so I got my things on and started to do a washing for Mrs B. I got three times water from the creek. Mrs Baltzell sat in the buckboard & drove, I dipped the boiler full, then I commenced washing for her. She had me eat breakfast there.

March, Wednesday 12, 1890

> I carried a letter to Liddell to have him send me a sum of money. I had a satin heart, brown & hand-painted, I carried it to Agnes Clibon, she 24 to day. Abbie 19, she has forgotten her mother. I cannot believe it. So cold this morning I nearly froze. I got the things ready & commenced washing.

March, Thursday 13, 1890

> My head aches, I am sick, did not get up till 8, Annis called to breakfast, I did not want any. I got, up she combed my hair. I sat down to read, soon heard Mr & Mrs Hoyt, they come to do that work. The *Beautiful story* & Stanleys book, Heroes of the dark continent, came today. I went at 3 to see if I could do anything for Mrs Baltzell, she in bed. I went and brought water, 2 big pails. Went to Ironing, such a lot. I got the supper, she so sick. Ironed till ten, the girls all so sleepy I made the bed for them up stairs. I stayed all night with her. Will I ever be so I can rest. God hasten the time, I pray. We got the three buildings moved all right—he away. Got 9 sacks potatoes, met *him* & Borden.

March, Friday 14, 1890

> I got up early, built both the fires, swept all the house, went to

Ironing. She got breakfast. Anna Brazelton came, 2 dresses. I then went, got Liddells check 10.00, I get my two under sets teeth. I hauled water for Mrs. B. Today Salleen cashed the check. All three of my prospectus ready, I worked all forenoon & then went home, got Ric all ready to go & get the things Mrs B. wants from her ranche, it a long ways out there. I got back at 4, it is a nice day, she so pleased. I got all, wash bench, stand, single bedstead, stove top &c. I carried them over to her. She got a cup of tea, I eat after combing my hair. I washed the dishes, then put the flour in her chest. Drove Ric then to the creek, watered her, then to see if Agnes would forgive me I could not come, yes. I went to see Mrs. Frick, she sick. I will wash for her tomorrow. We sat tonight by the fireplace.

March, Saturday 15, 1890

I up, eat a hasty lunch, fed Ric, put her in the pasture, went over to do Mrs. Fricks washing—she all humped up in bed with the cold. She tried to do a little & gave it up, laid down. I done some of my own in with hers, she awful afraid I would use a little soap. I hung the few things I could on the fence, the wind blew all down. I had them to do over, I hung up stairs, then I washed the dishes & cleaned the floor, sat down, put a band on her chimese, went to sleep in my chair, I so tired. I came home, sat by the fire-place, it so good. I try to enjoy the little we do have.

March, Sunday 16, 1890

We got up early so to go to John Sloans. I cleaned up Annis, she so verry dirty. I could not get ready till 9, then we started. I could not feel good towards her, it does seem she has done so much to injure me, she has always been a mischief maker, *all her life,* will be while she lives. I do believe now she nasties in her clothes, it is so hard to be patient. We got there about noon, she was getting dinner, a potatoe stew. After dinner we looked at the books, read & talked. He showed me the way I could go to Chas Mathews to carry his book. We had tea & buiscuits, prunes for supper. I helped nail the bedstead together, they had not scarce enough to make a bed. We slept both together, how hard to lay & hear her groan—

March, Monday 17, 1890

I got up at John Sloans, got old Ric with the halter, took her to the spring, she drank her 1 pail full. I brought 1 too the house. I combed my hair out by the buggy as she eat her oats. Then we had a little tea & buiscuits, they hard pushed. Annis *benastied* herself. *Oh dear* how do I get along with her. I cleaned her as best I could, then got Ric ready and started to go over a strange way to Chas Mathews to carry them the book, story of Man, for his survey of her land, the first I have sold. I do so hope I may get a few subscribers so I need not wash. 32 years ago today I eloped with the demon French. I am a free if not a happy woman once more. Canvased all the P.M., got Milk at Philipps, went to Mrs Holdens, staid. I found them all right, she washing—I put Ric in the stable, staid to dinner, buiscuit & peaches.

March, Tuesday 18, 1890

I up early, combed my hair, made bed, went down stairs, got 2 pails of water, swept the floor, did all I could to help Mrs Durkee, she so kind as to ask me to stay all night. A number of men there, Mr Elliott, John Starks, Mr Coons of Coons Crossing, they all seemed to want the books. One took the Beautiful Life, cheap edition. I went at the dishes for *both*. Soon we had them done, so much better to show a spirit to do something. They both was thankful, asked me to come again. The old mule eat up my oats, he gave me some more. I took Ric, on the way I picked up wood & coal, I watered her, come onto some corn fodder Purl foot dropped. I came back of Maxons, got my mail, a letter from Dannie. Over the hill I fell off, nearly broke my arm. Unloaded, got mush & rice Florence brought. Sent register $3.00 to Historical Co.

March, Wednesday 19, 1890

Up so to go to wash for Agnes Clibon at the Oaks home—I could not eat any breakfast so I turned the horse out, went over Mr Oaks on the way to the ranche. Agnes had the water on, I drank a cup of coffee, went to the washing, such a big one. My arm hurts me so bad, I got hurt in the fall worse than I thought, for I am sick, not able to wash.

March, Thursday 20, 1890

> I did not get up verry early—when I did I wrote awhile. Then I thought I had better change Annis bed, and while she is away to Sloans clean up her clothes. I put on the water, gathered up the things.

March, Friday 21, 1890

> Up early, did want anything to eat, fixed Annis pillows. I had washed the ticks, now they are all clean, so is her bed if it could only stay so. I went to patch for Agnes. I finished my new calico dress. Nearly finished my black stripe dress. Miss Ray the school-marm called. Mending piled all over, Agnes has her hands full.

March, Saturday 22, 1890

> Got up early, it so cold & windy, fed Ric, greased the buggy. I have to go & get Annis, she has been to Mrs Sloans since Sunday last. I will Canvass for the books as I go—I got hitched on, I nearly froze, took a quilt. Saw Chapmans boys at the creek, they filling in to change the course. Watered my horse. Met Old Mrs Baldwin, she said Mrs Jack Bal was over to Mrs Chapmans, they could not take the book now. I called at the house, warmed there, on to Mr Guilds, one gate to open, the rest open.

March, Sunday 23, 1890

> I got up early, went and fed and turned out Ric, then sat down to write. I thought I had better clean up and go to church. Self gave out there would be preaching on the 3rd sunday, that is today. I went. *None.* I went on to Mrs Baltzells—his sister and husband & the three children there from Falcon near Colorado Springs. She is verry pleasant, we all enjoyed a little chat. I read of the killing of *Benn Cline* by the cable on Welton Street. Mr B home & sick, he has done to big a job painting. He is a number 1 workman as my buggy testifies. I came home, the old cows all at the hay, they hooked a board off—I changed my dress, went & fixed it. Mr Oaks brought oats, Florence came, staid 2 hours. I let her catch old Ric, we were over there. Mrs Frick got a good supper, drove home.

March, Monday 24, 1890

> Annis fell down as she was going in the kitchen, waked me out of a sound sleep, I got up, got some breakfast, tea, rice, and bread, Florence brought it, the rice, while we were gone to Mrs Sloans. I got ready, went over to help Agnes mend. such a pile of stockings. Their Uncle Elrick, a brother of their father, came, also her sister, a Miss Dedrick from Empire near the Georgetown, she going back home. Agnes's stove pipe fell down as she was getting dinner, the meat all over the floor. I mended till 9 oclock, came home to the only home I have, the Frick house on the line of the RR. I brought bread and meat for us.

March, Tuesday 25, 1890

> Not one bit well, cannot eat, went to wash for Mrs Baltzell, the last I shall do at present. Such big days work, tis almost always a 2 weeks wash. I ironed till 9, she asked me to stay, no. She gave me some cold meat & bread. I got home, found Annis sitting by the fireplace so cozy. She tries sometimes to do a little. I rocked & rested, went to rest. This was so much better than to stay there, sleep on a hard cold bed up stairs with such selfish girls.

March, Wednesday 26, 1890

> I left the house nice & tidy, Annis can or dont clean up. I felt good this morning. I stoped & left a book for Mr Helgate to make one like it for Florence. He is looking for the Horse Roney so to shoe it. I paid $1.00, went on to see why Charley has not got him down from the ranche. I told him if he did bring him from his fathers, I should get him a nice Necktie. He had gone over to All Reeds. I carried the shawl & book over to Mrs B, went to see if I could not get some of the boys to go get the horse, I must have him shod sure. Charley asked Ric, I let him have her to go, he left her & brought Roney. I have to go & get her. I got done for a wonder at 4.30 P.M. Mrs. Whiting there talking to me so much I told her a few plain facts. She wants me to overlook all. I & Agnes went behind Roney out. Mrs W sent 2 turnovers to Annis by us.

March, Thursday 27, 1890

> I sick this morning—it snowed & so windy all night. I cannot go

today, had intended to start with the double team for Denver. I could not work I felt so bad. Done our breakfast on the fireplace, it so good, the salt pork I got. We let the storm rage—I nailed a piece on the side of the chimney where the snow came in, I got some wood in &c, then I fixed my black dress, also the rug for Annis she is to work on while I am away—about 6 I took the trunk down to the Depot for Dr Hig to take in *Sunday*. No Bible Prospectus come yet, will I have to wait. I got a letter from Olive & Dannie, he wants a nice piece to speak on Hunt, a learned time while on the ranche.

March, Friday 28, 1890

Up at 3, Annis has sat here all night, I thought she went to bed. I got up, went to getting things in shape, so if I can, must start though it is an unlucky day. I fed & curried the horses, found the hair that the Frick boys cut from Ric's tail & tied to the shalves sunday night, the little mischief. Put the breakfast on the old fireplace to cook. I am hurrying so to write this so it will not all be forgotten, I do get so far behind while I am working out for others. I do so pray for a rest from this, god can send it, he will, I have faith he will help us. I kneel at my bedside & ask it each night, can I be patient & wait—it is 9 we must eat *now*. I am so hungry. I hauled my buggy 7 times full of hay and put in the closet. I hauled an awful big RR tie, it all I could do to drag it to the cattle fence. I sent my weekly report, 1 book.

March, Saturday 29, 1890

Riches are not Forever, Rather set your heart not on the earth; but lay up treasure in heaven

Up so early, yet everything seems to stop me. I have tried for three days to go, cannot get started. here I went to sleep. everything I do seems to stand still. Dannies pants lie here for me to finish the band's. My brown check & black dress lay there to band and fix—Mr Taylor Green came in answer to sisters letter, he looked at her bill of Sale of the barn, thought it would hold it. He also looked at the Prospectus's for Story of Man, Stanley Travels, & Beautiful Story, would like them but must say *no*, had to get out of debt. I got in 19 pails of water for sister to use while I am gone to Denver. I got him to help put in the tongue in the buggy & I *greased* it. I sorted the potatoes, put them in the buggy, was tying on the hay, it was 3 ocl., here comes Grandma Kenedy to see us—I gave up going till Monday. She wanted me to write to her sister Sophia Grindol, Dalton City Ill. I wrote a good long letter, she was so pleased. I went to creek to water them, Roney lay down to roll, he could not get up, he is old without doubt, I have bought *him*. Myron 37 today

March, Sunday 30, 1890

I up at 5.30, sister slept in her chair last night. I had covered up the potatoes with new rug & carpet—it is so bitter cold & storming. I fed them, seem all right, *eat* good but I am still to wait. We got breakfast by the Fireplace & eat there cozy any way, if the storm does rage outside. Sister combed my hair, I am getting gray so fast. Oh how bitter cold it is, I cleared of the lounge and lay down, Annis reading out loud Phillida—in my Ladies Home Journal, such a nice book, I do wish I could take it and rest & read. I cooked some potatoes and mashed them, fried a piece of pork, we eat & enjoyed it—I went & changed the pail in the well, then I got the horses & watered them, they drank both of them, Ric & Roney, 9 pails in all. Then I sat me down again to write in my dear little diary, the holder of my poor thoughts and actions— may I yet record successes in my new employment—God be with & bless for *Jesus sake*.

March, Monday 31, 1890

How long wilt thou hide thy face from me, Oh Lord! Amen Stormy, so cold I got up. Annis wants to help me so much, but she is tired out. She lay down on the fireplace hearth & went sound to sleep this morning. I got up and made the fire, then we cut blocks to line the log cabin quilt that she is going to piece while I am away. She has made one for a pattern, such a mess. We will see how it will look if she ever does any more *to it*. I fed and watered *Ric & Roney*—it still snows. She cooked me some Oat meal & warmed the mashed potatoes so I could have some to eat. I made some tea, eat my breakfast, started at 10. I almost froze—I drove as fast as I could, got as far as Banks, stoped & fed—old

Mrs B so nice. I started on again, got lost beyond Elizabeth, went into a Mr & Mrs Peck's, the sister of Mr Tallman. I never was treated better, such hospitality, got 2 subscribers for my books.

April, Tuesday 1, 1890

I up early trying to get everything all right. Ric & Roney so poor as crows. Mrs Peck gave me a can of milk. I stoped at Mr & Mrs Miners. I got another subscriber and the directions on to the road to D.

[later:] April 24 when if ever will I fill this up, 3 in morning

April, Wednesday 2, 1890

Be instant in season, Oh Lord Lead me to the rock that is higher than I. Sewed for her & Cora, her hired girl, made near 2 dresses, played at cards with the family in the kitchen after the churning was done.

April, Thursday 3, 1890

Made the great mistake of my life, I feel it so clear, let Ric & Roney go for $75.00 for a small I guess part poney. Oh dear, I feel as if it was a big mistake now & I never have rode behind him till today.

April, Friday 4, 1890

The eternal god is my refuge, and underneeth are his everlasting arms Up at Mr Woodburys, he & his daughter Eva going with us, the potatoes he is going to exchange, get me some in D. She gave me such a little piece of butter, the first stingy thing I have seen her do. We all started at 8, the poor bargain I have made hitched in to pull us to Denver. I feel I have made a big mistake—Dan comeing from school as we drove up, so glad to see mother. We had feed unloaded in front of the house, got them some to eat. Then we went down, got her an album at Hardys, went to get my trunk, the check lost, had to prove & claim, got it in the buggy, went to Moores, got Olive a pair of shoes & rubbers—some hair dressing, home. [later:] I am sucked in $100.00 by George Pryor, Prince a horrid bribe.

April, Saturday 5, 1890

I lay enjoying the rest at home. Can I ever see the time when I
need not jump when 5 oclock comes. The whistles are blowing
but there is no school today—I must rest a little before I get so.
Sent my weekly report, 5 books.

April, Sunday 6, 1890

*They that know thy name will put their trust in thee. The everlasting
God! Amen*

Got up 6 ocl, this is Easter *morn*. I got 2 Doz. eggs last night of
Mrs Land, paid $14.00 grocery bill, such a bill for 2 too much. We
had a nice breakfast. Now must get ready for morning service. It
is communion, may God bless it to our good for Jesus Sake.
Olive, Dannie & I all there, side by side again—Olive fixed a
white lace cap for little Agnes so she could go with her mother.
She dresses in black, her little boy Lee died in Kansas. They
brought him here to bury, it cost them $100.00, his sickness &
death. We are poor together—we drove my new purchase Prince
down to church, he is such a good roadster. We were a little late,
had to take seats in the gallery, a good sermon. Christ is risen the
text, the church trimmed on the pulpit beautifully, the word Welcome woven of white flowers over the rostrum. We drove after
service to Mrs Curriers, she lying down upstairs, looks miserable.
Mother Temple there, she will do all she can for them. [later]: A
Mr Tomlinson here when we got home, he was the man that
moved us into this house. He has stoped drinking.

April, Monday 7, 1890

Got up verry early, Ollie so hard to wake up. She done well when
she did waken, got breakfast, finished boiling the beef. How I do
need some place to lay my head. She does need a dress to wear on
Arbor day, so I must try to look over the things & see if I have
something. I found the old summer silk that mother sent to Abbie, blue & white—shall I try to make dress for her out of it,
'twill be a job—I looked and planned till I was tired, it would
make a good dress but I am so tired of such old duds, why cant
we have something new to make. Dannie seems to be learning—
how I do wish I could get a good place for him where he would

be made to mind. They are both off to school. She combed my old head for me, I went just at eve for the milk. Saw on Long-fellows house corner (lots for sale), I went in. Now shall I swamp all we have, God forbid. I must do something.

April, Tuesday 8, 1890

In him we live & move & have our being! he strengthen us day by day.
I so sick with a headache this morning. Mr Larkins will do all he can to help me. I do hope he will stay with it, he could not go to work for the wind blows a hurricane. Towards noon it let up some. He will go with us to look for the lots, where shall it be—God help me. We looked at several. One pair for $500. We went to see about them on Champa, they are in the control of the loan Association, a dangerous organization for a helpless woman. I dare not touch them. We gave it up for the time, will go tomor-row I think. Ollie home & getting the supper. She is my life, the dear child. Will not some good fortune overtake us.

April, Wednesday 9, 1890

In him we live & move & have our being! he strenghteth us day by day
We all talking lots & a home, how will I succeed. Had our break-fast, Dannie got the horse ready so Luella & I can go to look at the Barnum addition and see if there is not some cheaper thing we can get. We went to 1616 Glenarm, Dr Buchtels office, had to wait for the clerk. He came, we went back to get a lunch so to go out with him this afternoon. He came, the clerk had him to turn Prince around in the back yard. He is so hard bitted. I changed my dress. I was so warm, put on a black calico with fans & buds in for fig-ures, white, we went on the boulevard, saw several but such a price, $75.00 the cheapest and so far away. Drove all around, went home, thought we would take Larkins out but he came so late we had to give it up. I went & unharnessed the horse, everybody in bed.

April, Thursday 10, 1890

All that will live godly in Christ shall suffer Persecution
We still talking about a home, the one thing to bee. I put on the water to wash such a big lot of clothes. I washed till noon, Sue

got dinner. I eat in her room, she hung up the lines all full—I still washing. Miss McGill, Dannies teacher came, had a nice talk. She has to suffer like all the rest of us. I cleaned the floor, so nice we all feel when everything is clean. Mr. Longfellow is I think trying to help me, he came to show a lot near to the place we are in. Old Carpenter putting in a pump now, after we have suffered all winter. We all went to see the lot just at dusk. Herb going to the encampment of the G.A.R.

April, Friday 11, 1890

I had a bad headache & did not get up early. Mr. Longfellow came to take me down to see the owner of the lot, a Mr Monchrieff, an old man, he used to be so well acquainted with father. I concluded to take it, he to furnish a clear abstract. I left my Gold watch with him as security, now I must work as I never did before.

April, Saturday 12, 1890

There shall be no night there; Lord restore unto me the joys of thy Salvation

Got up here in *Denver,* at 5 oc. had a hasty breakfast, started at 6, roads good, Prince feels all right, old Ric how I miss her. He ought to be all right for $75.00 and the 2 horses sure, what a simpleton I am at times. We got to Rowleys at 1, eat dinner, fed him, then I took a cross road onto the Elizabeth road so as to not go a mile out of my way—stoped a few minutes to get the harness fixed. He, the shoe maker Grebe, so buisy cant do it today. I went on, the wind blowing a perfect gale, has since 10 this morning. We got as far as bank's, the old Swigert place, the boys asked us to stay till morning. Dan did not want to, so we went on. Got near Elbert, met Elmer Colman the beauty, he is like all the rest only a little meaner. They all are trying themselves. I milked Mrs. Griffins cow she, Mrs G, is sick.

April, Sunday 13, 1890

Up not so early. I went to do the milking, she in bed yet, the cow bad to milk, I dont see how the little girl Tinna G. milks her as she does. I done the milking, got a nice bucket for doing it. She wants the watch bad so I let her take it. We went to Annis ranche, she was there all day, the old man paceing when we came in sight, he a nice old *feller,* she with him the old hag. I hear she is to have another by *him.* We went on, saw both the colts, also Wm Green, he to be a witness for Annis proving up. Came back, had a lunch, then went over to old Baldwins to see if Jack would not do the branding, he said he would. We came back, drove into Mrs. Geargia, they over to Mr Waldo's, had we known it we could have seen them. There it began to storm, we had to stay all night. We all, Annis, Dan & I, slept together in one bed.

April, Monday 14, 1890

Hold thou me up, and I shall be safe.

We up at 5, I got everything ready, horse curried & fed, for a start for home. We went to see Mrs. Hattie M Baldwin, she did not say it, but I believe he, *Jack,* dont intend to brand the colts. His mother is such an old blow. It cold and storming, we was not long getting down to the house, drove in and watered Prince at the creek, got home and some thing to eat. Annis knitting for Florence Frick a pair of stockings, we furnish the yarn. I left her a nice lot of wood, flour, meat, butter &c, she is getting along all right so far. I went to see Mrs. G and eat supper there. He so queer, she will have to work & earn the watch if she has it, she gave me some of her hair to get her a chain made. I milked the cow for Tinna, she is so verry brave. Emma Baldwin is working there, Mrs G fell and got a hurt in *the barn.*

April, Tuesday 15, 1890

Bless the Lord oh my soul, forget not all his benefits

Myron back, met him, Amias C baby born today. So cold this morning but I have to get those colts branded sure. I had Dannie to get the horse hitched, eat my breakfast, we started for Jack Baldwins, he would not get up for us. Dannie knocked & pounded—we went on over to the Father & Mother's, she soon let the cat out, they are afraid of their being some trouble. I & Annis own our colts, we have a right to do as we please, as much as we have with our wood pile. We went over to Guild, Lon Foots Brotherinlaw Knight—there he told us where to get a man, we sent back. Saw Jack up, went in, they willing when I said it was safe. I sewed up his Gum Coo [?] for Hattie, she soon to be confined. I think I gave him $2.50 for ropes & work. We got Annis, drove to Waldo, he at work on his new barn. I got some blocks, put Annis in her cabin, went found the colts, drove them in Will Foots corral. Jack built the fire, soon had the brand ELF on both Rock & Rody, lost a hitch. It snowed.

April, Wednesday 16, 1890

Whom have I in heaven but thee

We up early, Annis doing all she can to help us to get a start. Snow on the ground, the roads are so bad cannot start before noon. I went down to milk for Mrs. Griffin and carry the bridle home that she lent D yesterday. Mr Griffin came to his dinner yesterday, he said she could not keep the watch, today he says he dont care. She let me take some of her hair to get a guard made for the watch. She crochets so nice, she gave me milk for Annis— I went back, got us some dinner, then Dannies hitched up. We put in the lounge, a jar, screen, the horse feed, a load, yet not heavy. We did not try to drive fast, only on the level. Got to Nan W, I paid her some money to stay. We put the horse in the stable where Rip used to be while broke.

April, Thursday 17, 1890

We love him because he 1st loved us

Up at Nan Wests, she is good and doing well, oh how I wish *I* was. Mrs. —— Boston a dear little woman came in, she lives next door, had her baby in her arms—little does she know that he is so unfaithful to her—I saw her when she was first married. She has had twin boys and lost them since then. Dannie never told me one thing, that the horses back has got sore. Dan had in his pockets an old door knob. I threw it away, he is always picking up trash. We got as far as Mrs. Rowley's at noon, fed a good lot of oats. Had a good dinner, started right away, must make Denver to night sure. Prince played. Got here at 7, the horse so tired. Currier had been for me & I had Mr & Mrs L take me over.

Denver

The City in Spring

*Emily moved to Denver in the year of the city's greatest development,
during the climax of well-being and prosperity in the United States,
when the national wealth was higher than ever before. According to the
U.S. Census the population of Denver in 1890 was 106,713, up 60 percent from 1885. Some 2,500 people were arriving in Denver every month,
creating a shortage of jobs and housing. In 1890 Denver real estate agents
sold $65 million worth of real estate. Cable and trolley lines stretched out
past the city onto the bare prairie, which was platted in lots that would not
be built on, in some cases, for nearly half a century.*[39]

*Denver in 1890 was lively and exciting, the scene of parades and enor-
mous public picnics; balloon ascents and medicine shows; opera starring
Adelina Patti; and drama starring Barrymore. Under construction in the
city's center were brick and stone business blocks, substantial churches
and theaters; the streets were crowded with people, streetcars, horses and
carriages, with electric lines and even a few telephone lines overhead, for
Denver was up to date.*[40]

*Denver was one of a number of western cities that paid for rapid
growth with problems of crime and waste disposal, fire and disease, unemployment and poverty. Denver's homeless and jobless newcomers camped
in a labyrinth of tents and shacks on the banks of the South Platte River,
where sewage wagons poured filth under cover of night, and garbage wagons filled the river so thick with refuse that it hardly flowed. Petty theft
was rife; coal and feed companies hired guards to prevent constant pilfer-
ing of their stockpiles by poor people and hungry horses, such as Emily*

and her mare Fanny. And for the pleasure of men, women, and even children, 500 Denver saloons stayed open all night.[41]

When she first came to Denver, Emily stayed at Dan Larkin's house in Fairview, a district of small houses and small businesses, mostly dairies utilizing the waters of the South Platte River on the east. Fairview was close to downtown and connected to it by a new electric railroad racing along Colfax Avenue at 6 to 8 miles an hour. On the north end of Fairview were the Brinkhaus and the Jacobs additions, which Emily called the "Chene Dago outfit" (December 18) for their population of Jewish, Italian, and other immigrant groups. South of Fairview was the Wier addition; southwest of Fairview was Barnum, developed by the famous showman P. T. Barnum; and west of Barnum was Villa Park.[42]

The neighbors that Emily mentions in her diary were laborers and small businessmen: George D. Larkin was a plasterer living on the south side of Willow; Dan Larkin was a lather living on the south side of Monroe Street near Main. Jonathan Longfellow, who lived on the north side of Willow, was postmaster at the Colfax Post Office near Fairview; Frank Spencer was a switchman on the Denver and Fort Worth Railroad; Martin Cyphers of Jacobs addition was a carpenter; Charles M. Everett was a merchant and dairyman on Monroe at Main; G. E. Corbin and sons George J. and Llewelyn E. Corbin operated another dairy on Monroe near Main; Isaac Grewel was a teamster; John Epley and his sons A. E. and R. W. Epley were brick manufacturers in Jacob's addition; a man named Silverberg was a rag peddler living on Willow near Main; Edward McBride was a laborer south of Wier's addition; James Wier was a farmer in Wier's addition south of Fairview; Bernard Goldblat was a carpenter in Brinkhaus addition, living with Samuel Goldblat, a dairyman.[43]

Fairview is still there, bounded by West Colfax on the north, Federal Boulevard ("the Boulevard" in 1890) on the west, West Eighth Avenue on the south, and the South Platte River on the east. The street names have all changed; Willow, the street where Emily's house was, on lot 22, block 4, is now West Thirteenth Avenue. On the south side of West Thirteenth Avenue or Willow Street are several very old, story-and-a-half houses on 25-foot lots, but Emily's house is gone. Some old one-story row houses (called "terraces" in Denver) still standing at the end of West Thirteenth Avenue are probably Epley's flats.[44]

April, Friday 18, 1890
>   *This is not our resting place*
>   I had a poor bed in the chamber with 3 others, Mr Jackson the
>   first, the Sweed boy the second, I the third. I done the room
>   work, got dinner. I then went & got a powder box & puff for
>   baby, cost $1.50.—I have so little money but I am always giveing.
>   The woman that is washing her clothes fell down. A Mrs. Norton
>   came to wash. I took good care of Anna, the baby is a little trea-
>   sure. Anna does seem so happy. I am so glad she is doing well.
>   Mr Currier thinks everything she does is law, how nice to be so
>   well carred for. I never did have such a life—Olive drove over af-
>   ter her school, said I had to go & see about the lot. She staid, I
>   went to 1907 Arapahoe, the son there, I talked. The 2 lots in Uni-
>   versity I must trade them.

April, Saturday 19, 1890
>   *Who shall seperate us from Christ*
>   Up early, had breakfast, wrote three letters. Will I get my home,
>   god help me—Mr. Longfellow came to take me & close the bar-
>   gain. We went to see Judge Liddell, he always my friend. He not
>   in favor of my doing this, thinks the risk too great. I *must* venture
>   or lose all. We went with the deed of the lots I have in South Uni-
>   versity Place. I traded my colt Rip on the 16th of Sept 1889—now
>   this day I can let them go & save. So far this is good.

April, Sunday 20, 1890
>   *Can two walk together—except they be in mind agreed*
>   We got up to late to get any milk of the Corbins dairy. I went
>   over to see, she wants Olive to clean her floor once a week. She is
>   willing to do it—we cleaned us up, then sat down to read. Mr
>   Larkins & Dannie down for the mail, they came, we had early
>   supper, enjoyed the evening verry well together, to bed early.

April, Monday 21, 1890
>   We had got up early, I got the breakfast—let Olive commence the
>   pin cusion for that dear baby of Annas. We sat down to eat, hear
>   Edith is *old*. Carpenter with the men he has rented, he is mean to

try to crowd us up so—Luella felt verry bad. I tried to have her to down town with me. She was afraid Agnes was going to have the measels, so I went down alone. I got a paper from the land office for Sister, they say she is allright, no hurry, so I have that attended to. Then I went and left the hair for Mrs. Griffins chain. She has Anna's watch. How I hope something will turn so we can have a home. I got the spelling book for Mrs. West at Elizabeth as I promised her I should. 25¢, that for staying all night. I paid her 25¢ more, a good woman but like myself, so misunderstood.

April, Tuesday 22, 1890

Great is thy mercy toward me Oh God!

Slept oh so sound. I never heard the man Jackson when he came in. Mr. Currier had a fire when I came down. I set the table, cooked eggs, fried potatoes &c. Charly the boy that is liveing with Anna I called. He is a sleepy one, I called again. After Mr C went to his work, took his dinner. I done the work, clean the cupboards & put scaloped papers on the shelves, washed some for baby, made griddle cakes for dinner. After dinner got Anna up, she felt so much better. I made her bed &c, cleaned the kitchen window & the stove, got the clothes in that I had washed & I ironed them, a line full, pealed & mashed some potatoes, wrote a note to the butcher, Mr. Butler, sent the little Sweed boy Hialmar Bjork that is living here with them. I mended his pants, he is wild, no mother here. Some Salvation army girls called to see her, they kneeled and made a feeling prayer for her & the child, *amen.*

April, Wednesday 23, 1890

My strength & my redeemer

Up at 3, sitting in the little chamber & trying to write up since the 7 ult. So much has transpired, can I ever again get up. The cable wire has now commenced to run, here comes the sun, the days are so much longer. I left this, went down, found he had got his own breakfast, eaten & was almost to go. He had the plan of my shanty ready, changed it in heigth of room. I feel he will see the lumbermen. I got my breakfast, done up the work, washed & dressed baby Edith Isabelle Currier, nice, put the sweed boys lunch on the table, fixed a good fire, went on foot, no fare not a

nickle. I got there 10.15 a little late. Mr Longfellow there, now
for a *long pull* all together. I gave my notes, 3 to draw interest, 1
for 75 due April 23rd 1891, 1 Apr. 23. 92, 100.00, last 100.00 Apr.
1893. Can I ever pay this up, I shall try, I feel as though I shall
succeed.

April, Thursday 24, 1890

The Lord is good to all! and his tender mercies are over all his creatures
I must rise though I am so sleepy, this abused little Diary I shall
love to read in the future. I got a letter from the Hist co saying I
could go on with the canvasing. Now for it—I got breakfast,
boiled eggs &c, coffee, it raining hard, a bad day—I done my
work, here comes Mother Temple, she thought I would be gone
as I had to go to see to this business. She dressed the baby, we put
a raisin in the navle, it so inflamed. I got lunch for her, she one of
Gods chosen. Anna I got up to sit for a while, she with us now.
The dear girl is getting so smart, baby 10 days old, it is such a
bright little one. Mr Currier came home, he cannot work, it is
snowing, so he has a chance to buy a house for $40.00, such a
good thing for me. Rain & snow, a heavy fall, all day cold & dis-
agreable. I have to wait my house now sure.

April, Friday 25, 1890

I up early, the Sweed boy called to me to get him a pail, no, I have
orders not to wait on him—he is so lazy & impudent, he respects
no one. It yet snowing hard, has all night. The cable cars running
by Mrs Curriers are loaded down, the bells scarcely ring, they are
so covered up mud & slush, what a sign. Overhead is *white,* no
one can move arround much. I did up the work. Mrs Temple
came, she dressed the baby. She is like all the rest, *cranky,* knows it
all. I went up and cleaned the chamber so nice, picked up the
clothes, made the beds, swept the rooms, got a lunch for us all.
Mr C is good natured, no difference what the weather is. He got a
gallon of milk, made a custard, fixed his wine he made last fall,
offered us some, *no.* Mud knee deep. I came home to find Mr
Tomlinson there, he is verry attentive for some reason. I had all I
could do to get over from the viaduct, everything is swimming.

April, Saturday 26, 1890

> *We are bought with a price let us glorify God in our bodies which are his*
> Up and breakfast early, have to get consent to keep the kitchen, if
> they give the consent then I will let them have the room I have
> my things in. I went in to see them, Mrs Weber & Mrs Stuart.
> They seem ready to do right by us, now we must vacate the room
> and move a load over to Mrs Longfellows cellar, put all but the
> lounge in, it to large, put it in Mrs. Corbins attic, such long weary
> waiting to get a home, will I ever succeed, God grant—I went
> and took Olive over to Mrs. Curriers to help her while she needs
> it, she getting along nice. Mother Temple comes to dress *Little*
> *Edith, Louisa, Isabell,* she is hansome as a picture—I came on the 8
> oclock. Can we do this way? I got milk for our supper. Ollie has
> good bread, so much is nice. We set the big box of dry goods by
> the back door, if it rains we will have a strange mess—

April, Sunday 27, 1890

> I got up from the floor where we slept, we are so crowded, what
> will we do? If we can only keep good natured, we *will will* get
> along nice. I went at the work to get breakfast for us. I had meat
> & potatoes, Luella fried eggs, good coffee.

April, Monday 28, 1890

> Came in from Mrs Shirrells at 8 p.m., found Wayne Tomlinson
> and Dan Larkins. They have found a house and rented it. I cleaned
> all day, am verry tired.

April, Tuesday 29, 1890

> I went with the horse to have him shod. Olive stayed to help
> move, Luella & she packing the things. I put the girls plants into
> the Buggy so nothing can happen to them. They will be pleased. I
> drove around front of old Goldblatzs, such a low nasty place—

April, Wednesday 30, 1890

> *Slow to anger is great of understanding*
> Swept the parlor and the mens rooms. A Miss Ida Chittenden
> called with the Pros[pectus] Path of life. I went down to meet her
> at the St James, wrote a letter to Anna & Mr Waldo, she gave me a

stamp. I gave it to the bellboy. We went to her room, 1916 Curtis,
for some papers. I paid her $5.00 for the book & agency.

May, Thursday 1, 1890

Perfecting holiness in the fear of God
Washed a large lot of clothes for Anna C—could not hang them
out it so cloudy and wet. I put them in clear water, the boys sister.
The sweed came to sew on A's sewing maching. Staid to tea,
steak, potatoes, cheese, crackers, grape jelly. Mr Lundburg's
teacher came to get him a music lesson. They played verry nice.

May, Friday 2, 1890

Set your affections on things above, not on things on the earth
I slept so sound though I have such a poor bed, scarce any covers
on. I dreamed about Annas ranch. Hurried to get the fire built, at
5 got breakfast—eggs, coffee, bread, cheese. Got the clothes out,
washed 3 blankets for A. She pinned up my bonnet & vail, gold
glasses. She can spare me after today. I sent Olive to her on the
Cable. I went to see Robert S. Roe concerning the purchase of the
lumber, he sent me to Dea Levering.

May, Saturday 3, 1890

I went down town this morning to see what was necessary to get
the lumber. I saw the manager, Mr Bryant, of the Halleck &
Howard Co. He said if I could get 2 to sign a note with me for
$500, I could get the lumber, I to pay $45 in cash. I went to Deacon Levering, he signed as also did Robert S. Roe, the head men
of the church. I went, got the check of Liddell for $50, now what
shall I do. I drove home, fed the horse, went down at 2, made all
the arrangements for the delivery on the lot 22 in Block 4 Fairview addition of the lumber for the house. Now I must get all
ready sure. I took the caseings & windows to Joe Corrin's on
Champa—for him to fit & get in shape—came home, got our
supper. Wayne Tomlinson came, staid till 12, we had fun playing
old maid.

May, Sunday 4, 1890

*Like as a father pitieth his children, so the Lord pitieth them that fear
him. Amen*

Every one in a good nature. Mr Larkins out to feed the horse, he
not well, works to hard, has to haul water today for the men tomorrow. Fried the steak on the stove. We had a piece of mutton
she gave us, we are so poor, can we ever get a house, we must all
suffer & do the best we can. I cleaned the children up so nice. We
went in the buggy to church, such a good sermon on the crusified
savior, that he must have been cru[cified]—for 1 of six reasons—
either he was a Jew, Roman, Greek, fanaticle, criminal or Savior.
Went to Church & com[munion]—after to Anna Curriers, they at
dinner everything so neat & nice. We just called to see if he will
come and help put up the frame next week, the lumber to be on
the ground on Monday 3 P.M. Addie & Charley Q. came to see
Luella & Dan, her brother. It commenced to rain, I hitched up to
take them home, he would not let me, started off, so queer. They
are a tricky lot, have made a nice lot of trouble for others, his first
wife is *left,* for her, she is not true.

May, Monday 5, 1890

The heart grows weary when want stares us in the face, so little to
get breakfast, what will I do, nothing to encourage me in my
work, all wrong, up late, cooked some potatoes, made milk,
grava & old tea. Dannie not well, he not a strong child, he took
Ollie's book for her to school. She had brought a large book to
copy from. I worked at it for her saturday morning, she staid
home today. I sent her to have Dannie come back from school, to
go & have their pictures taken. She shampooed her head, we got
ready, drove the horse, went to Mrs Hirshberg to get Olives hair
frized. I must have their heads taken together in my watch. I gave
Luella my brown sateen dress. Addie came, Agnes has a hard cold
I guess, she sits & her eyes run. If it is, the measels dont show. I
went to the church study, took a list of names of a few members
to call on in my canvasing. Then come for Luella to go to the
Villa Park school to vote for a member of the school board. Mr
Fassett saw Miss McGill. I took Sue to Mrs. Webbers, the family
got the measels, she took care of them while Mrs. W. went to
vote. I come back, drove in front of carpenters, turned arround
the horse, turned down the bank, upset the buggy, cut my right
eyebrow and my nose. Olive so scart & put plasters on. So weak,
bled bad.

May, Tuesday 6, 1890

It doth not appear what we shall be! When he doth appear, we shall be like him

I got up at 4, Dannie so sick all night, vomited all over the bed. I gave him oil twice, he covered the floor. I changed his clothes. Went and fed the horse at 6, I have to go and see where the men at Halleck & Howard have taken it to. I eat our poor breakfast—potatoes, flour grava, good bread, coffee. I started at 7, went immediate to the office. He had sent all his teams out, I would have to wait an hour before I could get a team to go. I went to the P.O., saw Joe Carrin—said I could get the window caseing in a day or so. I went again then to see about getting the sewing machine. Then to see the man that lives next to my lots, he perfectly willing to move the rubbish off. Then came arround the "*Sheney* settlement, home. Luella ready to do I took her to the Fair, 16th & Champa, then to the lumber office, he ready at last, 4 times I went this morning, he put the load down all right. I had a long talk with Longfellow. I cam home so sick, I took 3 pills this morning, I gave Dan 2 pills, Olive 2, she took them good, she, Sue & Agnes took the express wagon, hauled Agnes over to Addies, *they full.*

May, Wednesday 7, 1890

Up betimes, so much to be done just now, the lumber on the lot yet no one ready to touch it. I will try once again if I can get anyone at it. I started at 9 to see about the finishing lumber for the roof, some must be bought. Longfellow says, *they* said they would send it sure. I went then to Chain & Hardys to see Mr Bancroft, their head man in the book trade. He not in, I waited from 11 till 2.30 P.M., then started home. I found a bunch of hay & a good corset. I gave it to Luella. I had no dinner, went to Mrs. Corbin, she gave milk, then to Mrs Longfellow, got a clean undervest, home to get a pail of water & find Luella in a tent with an Irish woman. She dont see how treacherous they are. I eat a lunch cold, nothing warm for a week. How long will I be able to stand it. I went again to see Longfellow if he could help, no, not able, his cousin & a broinlaw been to Sloans lake, no help. He took me to Mr Roger, he going to go at the frame in the morning. I went to see Mr King, he will help—Dannie and Olive so

sick, she vomited all over herself. I got a 15¢ lunch While I was
waiting at Joe Carrin for the frames to be done next door on
Champa & 15th.

May, Thursday 8, 1890

Pray one for another's The effectual Prayer of the righteous availeth much
I went to see the old scamp Sylvester, I don't see what we shall
do. The children all are sick, Agnes is broke out nice, Dannie does
nothing but vomit poor boy. I sent for the Dr to see them both,
Olive is so sick. Mrs. Tomlinson, Waynes mother, came. She
thought a hot bath & pack them might do good so I got water on
in the boiler, I got everything ready, Louella only visiting, no as-
sistance till I was alone. I put Olive first, she done well, took it
just as Mrs Tomlinson directed, then we let her go home, put
Dannie in by ourselves. Then when I sponged them off I went to
see Liddell, got $5.00 to pay the carpenters, went to see Bancroft,
he gave me the agt name on Stout St, saw C Roth, Mrs. Griffin's
chain done, $4.50, then to P.O., got a letter from the Historical
Pub co, got hay & chop for horse, butter 15, eggs 10, and oatmeal
25 for the children, then to lumber Co, got kindling & rest of
lumber for caseing, paid Mr Wright $2.50, Mr Rogers willing to
wait, a window stolen last night, so bad. I went down on a keg as
a seat so to bring up the window caseings, they not touched yet,
how mean.

May, Friday 9, 1890

Up with Dannie till 3 this morning, he no better, Olive some. I
sent for a Dr again, Mr Hart in Platte Park came, he thought Dannie would get along all right—He wrote a prescription. I went to
the Golden Drugstore, had it bill, he trusted me. Went to Mrs.
Shirell to clean, now I can begin to pay my honest debts again. I
worked all day hard, I got a lunch at 11, cider, bread, cheese,
blackberries. Took out the carpet, dusted & cleaned the wood-
work, moped the floor. I sewed the carpet over so it will be all
new again. Ida got supper, greens, roast pork, tea, potatoes
mashed, rye bread, jelle cake, Doughnuts, so good. I can work
better when I have something to eat, now I shall get it done, put
the things to place. She gave me 10¢ to go on the cable to see Pat-

sey Heferon at the Liquor Store of Clark & Walker 1536 Larmier. I walked down, I so hard pressed—saw him come home, fed Prince, it raining.

May, Saturday 10, 1890

It is I, be not afraid, We have an advocate with the father, Jesus Christ Hart Dr here today. *Poor Ada's birthday.* Up all night with Dannie so sick, he took to bleeding at the noes at 5 this morning so hard. I got the horse ready to go for the Dr, he gone to the train for a friend. I went to get all the help I could to finish the house. Then to the lumber office to get a transome for the chamber, then to the Paint store on Market 1929 Howard & Co., got 1 gal for the roof, a brush. To Tritches, changed the lock for a better one, got a granite stew pan, gave it to Sue. I went to Addie's, got my gossamer, told her how bad Dannie was with the measels. I came home, they eating dinner. I had got the two windows after waiting all the forenoon, then he charged 3.00. I had given him $1.00, had to go to borrow it. I went to C. Roth, he not in, then to the Larmier St. Liquor store to see Patsy Heferon if he could let me have $2.00, no, had not it, & went back, got $2.00 of Roth, went got the frames, told Corrin he would not make much by this deal. I came back to go get finishing lumber, got it here at 3, brought a load of kindling. Dannie all right, broke out good, he will be well soon. Mr B asked me if I would be home on Sunday.

May, Sunday 11, 1890

I slept all night with my sick boy, he better this morning, ate some toast and drank tea, we had boiled meat, oatmeal. Wayne here at 9, he likes to come here for some reason. We sat outside, Agnes so cross, I came in & tried to get her still, then took this dear little book. It had to drop in a pail of water that stood in front of the cupboard—Dan Larkins acts as if all I had belonged to him. Wayne Tomlinson here to, I sitting and watching Agnes & Dannie, the measels out on her, not on him so well as yesterday. They on the porch fooling, how I wish Ollie could have a little sense not to be so foolish with old Larkins, he means no good. I let them take the horse & buggy to go for a ride, they to get back so I could go. They were gone 2½ hours, it 6.30 when they came

back. I would not go then. Lou ashamed but she has as much
meanness as he has, only she is cunning enough to hide it. I am
going to leave the whole of them, see if I dont. I am tired of doing
without thanks.

May, Monday 12, 1890

*He said unto me: my grace is sufficient for thee: he giveth power to the
faint Amen*

Cleaned for Mrs Sorrel, her middle room, took up the carpet,
turned and sewed it, cleaned the windows, all looks so nice. I got
her washing, 45 pieces, a tub small, some tins, went got the horse
to bring them. It rained so hard. I went to all the men to get them
to finis the house, went to the Halleck paint to get 1 gal roof
paint—hauled 2 14 [sic], some 10 pieces 2 x 4 changed the lock
for one with 2 keys, a good one, got 5¢ meal at the Packing co. I
could do so well if I only had a little money, oh dear, bought the
old tent of Mrs. Boulan, she lent me 2 50¢ pieces, 1 to give him,
the other for the old jew, he put a new seat in the kane rocking
chair, he is an old miser, they fight so all the time. I got Mr. King
a 50 lb sack of flour, some lard 5 lb, 45¢ coffee, 30¢ for ourselves.
How I wish I could get some work. I got Prince 2 bails hay, owe
now $2.50 to Terry. Mr McBride painted part of the roof. I had a
few ugly words from Dan Larkins, I will

May, Tuesday 13, 1890

I up betimes, such a roar as Agnes does make every morning, this
morning her rubber ball is lost that I gave her puppy Bounce,
bothers her altogether. She is a most unhappy child, just as her
mother is most of the time. I shall not be with them many days
more. Lou is hiding all she can. Moved a load in the buggy up to
the house, got more red paint, $300 in all, how it counts up. Will I
ever get all paid up. *God help* one to do just right with everyone
whether they do the same by me or *no*.

May, Wednesday 14, 1890

*Unto him that loved us and washed us in his blood be power forever!
Amen*

I up and trying to make a fire so Larkins can throw his steak on to

the top just this once more. He has an idea we have to stand all he
sees fit to do, he is so filthy in the house, today ends it sure—I am
going to leave with my children, my goods, all everything. Now
she sees that she has to make curtains, she has the old strips of
muslin Mrs Howell gave her off the chicken show coops. I will let
her take the sewing maching to help get her work done. I got all
my things picked up. At 4 John Nelson a sweed liveing at the
Boulans, next house where I staid Monday night when Larkins
acted so nice, Nelson loaded the wagon high, put all but the little
heating stove on and my boxcupboard & a few other small things.
He unloaded them at my house, a Mr Baldwin helped, got his
white shirt blackened from the cookstove. Nelson went with me
to Anna Curriers to get the trunk, carpet & bed, got there at dark,
put the bed up. [later]: little Tom staid with me at the house, only
1 third the roof on, half the floor. It rained hard ½ the night, we
got so wet. Larkins a good one, his word no good.

May, Thursday 15, 1890

I eat my breakfast with Mrs Boulan, she suffers so from the
drunkeness of the men, nothing does them but beer all the while.
It still raining. Larkins tore the shelves out of our cupboard, the
top off to use on his table, he is a good one after all I have done
for them. The old jew put my little stone in his old place he locks
his stolen goods in. Goldblock is his name, he is an old devil. I
told him he better get it out in a hurry or I would have his old
place searched. I went down with the stove frame & stove to get it
riveted. Frank Tritch gave him a zinck. I went to Stuckfields for
the riveting, he gave me 2 pieces of pipe, I got 5¢ meat, I paid 25¢
on a wringer, it 2.50, how I need one. Now we wont have to
move around I must have a few things. I went to the county com.
to see if they would help sister to get here on the cars, *no,* they
feather the rich, poor may suffer. The water co has the hearing,
the money goes there.

May, Friday 16, 1890

*His name is above all others' unto him shall ever knee bow and every
tongue confess*
We all feel so much at home, now the hamering is done, the

roof all on. Olive trying to fix things up, I helped her with the hard lifting till noon, then to see if I can get some work. I shall certainly suffer if I cannot. I have so many little debts that must be paid. Mr McBride came to do the rest of the roof. I had to get more roof paint, $3.00 in all, this one more bill that waits for settlement. Came home, he had his dinner with us, he lives on Argo St. near 19, a long distance. I gave him several pieces of boards to make some signs for washing & board, they have to work for a living. Olive put the carpet down so nice, Dannie helped her good. We are now comfortable, can make a live I do hope. I have always had enough to keep from starveing, will God desert me now, no, I believe.

May, Saturday 17, 1890

Got up early, had a nice breakfast with my children, every thing nice & clean, we can live nice if we all try our verry best. We must all earn some, by care I hope now to save a house, if it be poor then I will have only my taxes to pay—I have all these years tried so hard for one. Olive is trying to help though it be little. Went to clean Mrs. Sorrell's old red & black carpet, het water on the stove outside. She has her room arranged nice with the chineele curtains arround, and at the door white musketo net, it looks so clean & nice. I went home to get ready for a trip down town, found some sugar that had been spilled on the ground, took up near a cup full in the bottom of my blue dress. Come on the old Mrs. Langdon, look as if she would eat. I sent a letter of credit signed by Seaman, went to get the Photos of the children, they not done, I so disapointed, told him I would wait 1 more week—went to settle with the Howard & Halleck Co, they too buisy to day. 21 shingles.

May, Sunday 18, 1890

Let us not be desirous of vainglory

We feel so well all of us, we will have to go to church. Dannie out to feed the horse, I got 2 bails of hay $1.70 yesterday, it is nice to have the horse but it costs to feed it. We got to church just as they were singing, Dea Levering met us in the hall, I told him I was in the new house they had helped me to build, they seated me in the front seat, Old Mr Rease in seat. The Rev Dr Cooper of the 1st church of Richmond Va Preached on our Faith & works, is a thoroughly practical man, his sermon a good one—will preach at the Calvary Baptist cor Stout & 27th to night, I think I and O. & D. will go. We drove over, was on time but the church not lit up the Electric Lights refuse to burn. Candles & lamps in great demand, suddenly the lights come out just as the service begins—Hope & Charity the theme for the eve, he handles with a master hand, we shall some time see & be all satisfied, amen & amen.

May, Monday 19, 1890

Charity envieth not, seeketh not her own.

Up betimes, will eat a hasty breakfast, have to clean for Mrs. Longfellow today, must try to pay as fast as I can. Had to change Daniel underclothes after his measels, he is liable to get cold. His eyes are weak now, I had to hunt up my Brown curly pup Dash, I think the jew Goldblock has poisoned him, he dont seem well—I went at 8, not a good beginning for monday. I went to takeing up her carpet, it is a good three ply ingrain Green white brown black, a handsome thing, some yellow—leaves & vines. She is going to have the front room painted, how nice to have a kind husband & home, I have always craved both but alas they are not for me I fear. I washed a large one, hung out the clothes, cleaned the doors & transomes, the kitchen floor, came home to supper. Ollie got Mrs Shirells rake, I cleaned our yard. Just as I was done here come John Nelson that moved us up, he was full of beer, wanted to help Ollie make *garden*.

May, Tuesday 20, 1890

The foundation of God standeth sure.

Eat breakfast at 5.30 so to go to Mrs Longfellow to clean the window & wash curtain, they at breakfast. I stood in the yard and watched the tin bucket brigade go by, so many, the city is full. I went at any cleaning I dont feel well but must work all the same—I scraped the outside of the glass with a knife to remove the dobs of paint, helped put her beds out, made good suds, put the curtains through, they look nice. Lou Larkins down at the old Irish woman's gossiping as usual. Left at 4 oclock, must go and see if I can get work of the church society. It was given out on

Sunday that a family needed work, will I get the $4.00 to pay on the 3rd of June? God is able to help me, let me have faith I pray. Ollie home from school, she does enjoy this poor home, watered her house plants, she has a lovely Rose Geranium, also a red fish Geranium, a snowball gerenium, some baby tears. Her bird was killed by a cat.

May, Wednesday 21, 1890
> *The Lord knoweth them that are his.*

Was called out of a sound sleep at 3 to go to a Mrs. Bradleys on the oposite side of the street to lay out a child 5 years old. It had the "La Grippe" in Kansas in March, went into a decline. They came here three weeks since, seem to be nice people. They love their beer, so many drink that it is the curse of the workingman. They have plenty, I have scarce enough to keep soul & body in comfort, "will it ever change". I come with a word the children sent. Mr King is come, wants a trowl to build the wall. I got 1 of Mrs Rogers, lives in the back part of her house. I eat breakfast with her, I come, had to haul mortar & brick. Poor Prince, he is not half fed, is cribbing to death. Told Dannie to come for me so I can go with him to Prayer meeting. I went to help Mrs. Rogers, the carpenters wife had taken her to town in my buggy, a Mrs Oleson sweed was, there she went with us, had to be taken in a saloon to get a drink of "Port". Dannie did not come, I had to get a Mr. Dimmick till midnight to hunt, went to the Police, what does the boy mean to run of so.

May, Thursday 22, 1890
> *We know not what we should pray for right.*

Got up early, Tom Boulan asleep on the lounge, he is 9 years old, has no mother, lives with them. He went with me to hunt for Dannie last night, now I shall have to go with Dannie to the Chief of Police. I told them I should let them know if I found him with the horse, how strange for him to go off over to the church without me—he is a verry strange boy, yet I can see he does not mean to do wrong, he acts so like his old father. I went to Chief Farley, he said try the boy again. I went from the City hall to the P.O. in the Gettysburg Building on Champa & 17th, no mail, to the Fair

to see if I can get him a place. Saw & had a long talk with Wima
Tarbell, he has grown so manly, would that my own boys were
like him. They will see if they cannot make a place for Dan. Then
to the Rev Tupper to see if I can get work, not yet, will try to be
patient. Commenced Ollie cream silk that Mrs. Abrams gave her.
I shall try as never before to make Dannie see that I love him, I
have always been so kind to him. Ollie is so cross at times.

May, Friday 23, 1890

The spirit is willing indeed but the flesh is weak.
A few boards for overhead. Up early, Ollie helped me with the
washing. She hung up most of the clothes before school. I had
three dresses & a shawl, several skirts, a large wash, got through
at noon, had bread and milk for my lunch. Just now Wayne Tomlinson came to see about the story Dan Larkins had told that he
Wayne had lived somewhere with a woman, I told him I knew
nothing concerning him or his mistakes—I got Ollie's light silk
dress out to see if I could do anything to it, there is so much
needed to make it nice—the painter came to finish the roof, I
cleaned the pails out, got covered with red paint. He is going to
get a lot of odd kinds and put the priming on. Mrs Bradley, the
lady I laid out the little girl for, came over to see me a while, she
is so lonesome, only 1 child left now. Ollie came from school, she
wanted to go with Lena Cook over to Maud Hurd's, they gave
Ollie some vines, she planted them at the front North window,
put a little pink bow and a white cloth at the transome up stairs.
Emily's birthday 23 if liveing.

May, Saturday 24, 1890

*If we confess our sins he is just to forgive and to cleanse us from all
unrighteousness*
I cannot lie in bed after 5, got the fire for breakfast, Ollie up, fixed
the floor overhead, put the large cot up stairs for Dan to sleep on.
She likes it up there, wish I could finish the house up but I am so
thankful to get it enclosed. We cleaned the carpet & rugs, cooked
the beans for sunday. I went over to get some sour milk for a
cake, Mrs. Corbin so clever, she would have me take some of her
Hostellers Bitters, it is a medicine yet—I took it to please her, I

came home made the cake, had no sugar. Ollie & I ironed all, now how I do wish I could keep the work, everything as nice as we have it. Here comes Mrs. Corbin with a pail of sweet milk. I showed her the silk I am fixing for Ollie, a light cream, 'twill be a lovely dress! Next Friday is Deckoration day, she wants to look nice sure. Mrs C wants me to come over to get some cake & bread she has for us, all right. I got a few boards. Dannie went 2 like a man & took the horse to feed. I dont see unless something occurs how I am to live.

May, Sunday 25, 1890

We are all not feeling well. I must rest. Ollie got breakfast so nice, then she & Dannie went to let the horse pick grass, staid all the rest of the forenoon. I put Dash out doors, he dont act as if he would live. I know the old Jew's have poisoned him. I got a lunch for us, then sat down to write up a week in this dear little book. How I can remember and always could, will it always be so? I see all that happens arround. I gave Dannie a bath, a clean shirt, socks &c, then he went again & took Prince, the Old Cribber, how I was fooled by Mrs. Woodburry, she may have thought he was all right. Ollie took Ammonia & shampooed my hair and then combed & cleaned my poor old head. She grows more kind as the days go by, there may be rest for me yet. Now I must do a little to prepare for evening service, I think we will go to night, why not? God be with us & bless the service to our good, will he help me *do*?

May, Monday 26, 1890

The heart is deceiptful above all things; yea and desperatly wicked
I went to church last evening—was in session for the young peoples meeting I think we will join it, so much is derived from the true study of his holy word. How glad I am every day that I have chosen to serve my Lord and saviour. The sermon was to do good unto those that were our enemies. How strange that Mr. Lawson should hunt us up to get his sewing & mending & washing done, yet last evening while we were at supper I saw some one at the kitchen door, I was feeding my sick Dash bread & milk, I went out to see if he wanted anything of us, I dont invite men in, yes,

he had seen this little new house, inquired who lived here, he was told, came to see would I take his work, yes, too glad to get it. Larkins goes by here altogether to frequent, I think. I had to get dinner for Dannie, he is sick today. I have sewed some, he has to go out with the horse to let it eat grass, I can get no hay. Oh if god has other things in store for me let him make it manifest, I am at a loss to understand.

May, Tuesday 27, 1890

Up at 5, how I do hope I may get some work to do today. I got breakfast, made up the bread. Mrs. Corbin not feeling able to have the cleaning done. She is not a strong woman, I went to see if I could not help her, yes, I may wash the dishes & get the dinner. She gave me a nice lot of bread, some cakes, 2 pieces of pie, pickle feet, eggs, a little sugar &c, milk, all does help me so much. I had 5 loaves of bread made, had to make a fire, leave them to bake. I done her work all right, she gave me $2.65, how good, where could I find another to do more. I shall surely get the $4.00 to pay on the note, if I only had a steady employment. I came home to go down to Terrys to get hay, went to Posts to get the photos of the children, they not all done. I hurried home, went to get the supper for Mrs. Corbin, she not so bad, her head some better. I cooked the steak for the men, she & I had our tea in her room. While eating Dannie came, said Mr Lawson had come, brought *his work*.

May, Wednesday 28, 1890

Let us clean ourselves from all filthiness of the flesh as Christ is pure
I went as soon as we had our little breakfast, coffee, toast, the meat Mrs. C. gave us. I got cream, a pail of milk, took the horse Prince to feed over by the viaduct. I got a lb of coffee for Mrs. King, went carried it to her, saw Mrs. Price, her tent is on the way. She told me that Larkins had gone into the small house of Howells. I came by Mrs. Corbins, she at work. I went in, helped her wash the dishes, got a pitcher of milk, came home, eat my dinner, washed Mr Lawsons shirt, cleaned his pants, cleaned a water pail. Larkins stoped and introduced his Brotherinlaw Ell Von Osdell, must think I want to see them. I told him I must have An-

nie's quilt, that our Puppy Dash was poisoned, he did not seem to know anything about it, called me Auntie. I am sewing on the pants for Mr. Lawson. The children have just come home from school, Ollie has a lot of ink rings on her fingers. Sent them to feed the horse grass. I want to go to Prayer meeting to night, God bless & save me, even me. Olive sees her mistakes, she enjoyed the meeting so much, we are all benefited, god be praised *amen*.

May, Thursday 29, 1890

I up early, so much to do, something all the time, even though it is to pay my debts. I have the shirt to wash, made a fire & some starch as I got the breakfast, bread, cookies & coffee, may we always have so much. I helped the children of to school, then to mending Mr. Lawson's pants. They are so badly to pieces I have nearly to make them over. Worked as hard as I could all day. Olive came from her school, she is learning a piece to speak on the last day, a Revolution sermon delivered just before the battle of Brandywine.

May, Friday 30, 1890

He that wavereth is like a wave of the sea & tossed with every wind— Up at 4, Decoration Day, can I ever remember the half. I had a terible time to get to A, she washing just a little. Walls of brick all arround now. I went to Mrs Samson that brought her, so many nice things she lent me for the baby Edith. I got home at 5 so tired. I found again fathers grave, put snowballs & yellow roses on it, washed Mrs. Corbins dishes.

May, Saturday 31, 1890

Went first to get the stuff to add to what I already had to put on a small room for the hay & tubs &c, got 1 door all painted, 75¢, so nice, I put in the tent for the horse to bruise, I dont seem to think anymore. Mr King & Mr Cyphers to try to get the little room done to set things in soon.

June, Sunday 1, 1890

Jesus saith to Thomas "reach forth thy hands and touch the pierced side Not up verry early, coffee for B, not much else, some day perhaps. Went to communion a little late, sat in the galery, the text on the reality of Christ. A deacon with a large head gray passed to us the bread but gave us no wine. We went to church evening, the love of Christ ably handled Rev. Phelps, the assistant Pastor, opened by prayer, he is to be ordained thursday eve at the Boulder St new B.[aptist] church. Olive wore her cream silk first time to day, it looks so nice.

June, Monday 2, 1890

Up at 4 to early. I got some broken pieces brick, up at 4 to early. Some men came, wanted to get a load of the dry manure, I let them. Larkins came to talk, I dont want no more of him. I gave Ag a book. I took 2 small bottles to Sniverleys 5¢, went with Dannie to the Photo, got the pictures stuck in again, then to H. & H. to get the boards for a rough kitchen. Prince pulls all right if he only did not do as he does. I did 2 hours work in 1, such a hurried life I live, no rest. I brought a load—door, window, some 2 by 4, hay, a big load. Mr. Lawson comes here quite often. Mr McBride to dinner & supper. I got up while the painter had the ladder up & cleaned the small 1 light in front, then he eat dinner, it is all I can pay him now. 11 to bed.

June, Tuesday 3, 1890

Forgetting all those things which are behind: reaching out for those before
I up at 5, dressed to go to Mrs. Nickols on Hunt St. beyond the Green Broadway cars turn table. She so glad to see me, wanted me to get out of the buggy, go hitch and stay all day, no. I gave Pearl the ring on my little finger, she so pleased she gave me a boquet of yellow & Marshal Mil roses. I drove over to Anna Currier, on the way stoped to see Mrs. Fair, she in own house, washed Mrs. Corbins dishes. I got such a headache, she gave me a nice piece of her roast, so nice. I got dinner for the painter. I had to lie down, so sick, could not sit up scarcely. He painted the doors. Mr Simmons told me to go on Larmier & get the oil to put on the first coat. The painter will do it for $4.00, I will have it done. Ollie & D. trying to be perfect on examination. Mr. Lawson came as he promised, let me have $3.00 to make my payment, he staid till 10, why?

June, Wednesday 4, 1890

I hurried breakfast, could not eat. I have to go to Mrs. Grewells to do her washing, found I had to carry the water. The wind blew a hurricane. I had to go to the lumber yard for nails & putty.

June, Thursday 5, 1890

Washed for myself a large one, had four men's washing, pretty dirty. I commenced to wash Annis quilt, it verry dirty. Mr John Lawson came, he seems to take more than common interest in my affairs, how kind he is—I do begin to love to see him, I wonder what he comes for.

June, Friday 6, 1890

How nice I feel this morning. I seem to have an intuition that he loves me, he has not told me so but I know it, I feel it and I am so happy. I will await the issue. Went to Liddells to draw the last money he holds of ours, $10.00. Went to my dearest friend here, left $9.00 with Anna Currier's. Lundburg will get Olive a good guitar, better than I could. They that take the sword shall perish by the sword, prophetic, Ollie's school closed this P.M., she had her piece so nice. Mr Beatty had left the book at home & she had no way to receive help if she should fail. She did well.

June, Saturday 7, 1890

Up early, Dannie made a fire. I am feeling so verry bad I can scarcely get up. Ollie dont ever like to get started, she will do all right when she is awake. She is awake. She is so hard to get up. We had coffee, fried bread, rice. I swept off our floor, it is so nice now that we have it oiled with linseed. We can keep so nice. The flies have got in so thick since McBride began to paint, I am so glad it is all done. Now when I get all the little bills settled we can get something ahead to live on. I got 5¢ meat, 10¢ broken crackers, 10¢ dust pan, 75¢ ribbon, 1 piece pale pink satin ¾ inch to trim her dress, white shalley, I washed it, was basteing on the ribbon, had not had our supper. Here is Mr Lawson, I sat down to chat, Ollie so full of her fun, we had warm pie apple, tea cakes &c, he eat with us. Oh how can I ever write the rest, he loves me, declared it, I never can forget the good night kiss, will he be true,

he is a man of honor, yes I do love him! Oh such joy a I seem to
be away by my self.

June, Sunday 8, 1890

I lay thinking till near morn I am so in love with this man? will he
love me in return always, I shall be so happy if he does—on my
knees I asked God to bless us if it be all right, the love of a pure
woman is priceless. I got breakfast, the children got off on the ½
past 8 cable to Sunday S[chool], the first since Dec. We have been
so moved around, now we are in our own home if we can pay the
amount. God grant we may. I drove over to the church to morning service, Psalms 17–15. I shall be satisfied when I awake in thy
likeness—a good heartfelt sermon, though he was not well, had
to read from Miss. Came home, got partly changed, here came
Mrs. King I chatted with her, let her have a tea pot, we had fried
potatoes, lay down, had a nice sleep. Ollie had one of her ugly
spells, all because I asked her to sign the active members card for
the Christian Endeavor.

June, Monday 9, 1890

The triumphing of the wicked is short.
Up 5½, dont feel so well, my head aches bad. I got Dannie &
Olive up, he built the fire, she made & baked some griddle cakes.
We had boiled meal, tea. I carried water so she could wash some
while I went to sew for Mrs. Grewell. I went at 8, found them
getting ready, the boys to wash, she all so exausted with her
asthma, she is such a sufferer with her disease & so many children,
how thankful I ought to be that so much of the worries of life are
over. I seem to be able to endure. Christ has promised if we are
faithful to him we shall have the victory over death, hell & the
grave. Will the man I hold dear come soon, I wate with hope &
fear both intermingled. God knows best & *guide me.* I am waiting,
he has not come, what can be wrong, perhaps all for the best. I
read the 46 Psalm and had a long season of Prayer, Jesus my dear
saviour more precious *day by day.*

June, Tuesday 10, 1890

As Christ forgave you so also do you =

I slept good, felt so much refreshed, got up at 4, went to work mending, I can only think what is *wrong*. I called the children, Ollie got up, got breakfast, soup with dry crusts. I thank god I can have even so much, I may have even less only for faith I should give up! God help or I die. I am weak, not able for so unceasing a struggle. He will help me, I have trusted all these years, some times it is so verry dark. I carried water to wash Annis quilt that Mrs. Larkins used all winter, it is so verry dirty. I put those drawers that were so dirty, they are for one of the men in the next house. I wish I could get more to do, I washed the Star quilt that Annis gave me for a gift on my 45th birthday. I helped Ollie fix the floor up stairs, then we went to work on my black silk. I have had it partly made 1 year. I am waiting, *will he come,* yes, this night ever to be a remembrance in my poor life, yes, I am his promised wife, he shall be a husband chosen, I am happy.

June, Wednesday 11, 1890

> *Behold I make all things new.*

And I can scarcely contain the thought, am I realy loved for the first time in my life—I so craved it now it is mine pure and true. I do try to not be foolish, I am in a new life. Sewed for Mrs. Grewell, got nothing but a little bread today but I live in a new life. I am happy as I never expected to be. Ollie went to help Mrs. Currier, Dannie took her in the buggy, she is to help her for a week while I go to the ranche for Annis. I must bring her again into my life, only for trouble I fear. She has a terrible tongue and a worse temper, but since I have undertaken to see to her she does a little better.

June, Thursday 12, 1890

> *Being dead to sin, we put on the new.*

Mr Huntington came for me to go help his wife, she sick all night. I done the work—such a dirty hole, food thrown every where. Dannie at home alone. I got some of the cooked beans & carried to him, I could live so nice out of what they waste. He came again to night, *why?* Can I be contended with *him, yes.* I sat waiting for the 1 of all to me, Mr. John Lawson came, we were so

happy for three hours but we must part, he to go to his mines, I
to Annis. We went to the horse

June, Friday 13, 1890

Dost thou believe on the son of God, yes Amen with all my heart—
Martha
Went down to the general P.O., got the word that the Books were
at the Rio Grande Freight, had been since last tuesday. Had a long
hunt for the Depot, got them 50¢, got Dan a hat, washed all the
afternoon 5 men's wash. The wind blew hard. I went to see Miss
Miner, the lady that taught Ollie in the Boulevard School, she is
one of my sub's [subscriptions], the last. I rode after Prince, Mr.
Larkins came to trade him, I let him go.

June, Saturday 14, 1890

Went got some kindling wood, Dannie trying to make a fire. He
can scarcely ever get on. Commenced to clean my own house before time to go to work. I must have a clean house anyway, it is a
part of my life. Cleaned for Mrs Corbin, she is a woman after my
own heart, the kindnesses she has bestowed will *never never* cannot
be forgotten. Cleaned some for the Jews, next house. I cleaned
and papered my own old cupboard, mended the mens wash, got
me in a clean dress so good. I sat and waited, Oh will I have to do
this always? I am tired, 1 ocl. Oh dear, what is the fault if any old
carpenter I guess

June, Sunday 15, 1890

God hath called us unto holiness—If ye have faith like as a grain of
mustard
I let Dannie sleep. I got up at 5, got a chance to read & write
some. Soon got him up, he is so cross, just like the father. He
built the fire, we had fried bread, coffee cake's thanks to Mrs Corbin. She remembers me so often, bread, how can I repay. I
cleaned, yes she will pay ½ doz times—now we will go to Sunday
Sch. I got ready in time without any confusion, wore the brown
silk, saw Mrs. Osborn the dear soul, she remembers me. I have
not seen her for 18 months. Oh how full they have been to me of

worry & deep trouble, God is raising the cloud—after church I
drove over to Mrs. John Nickolas, a warm welcome, eat dinner,
came back to church, the Sunday closeing, Rev Swift came down
18th, watered the H, came up the Boulevard. Dannie wanted to
go on to Sloans Lake so we went, the wind awful. Home, will he
come 9 *oc, no*. Why does he not come here oftener, I am so lonely.

June, Monday 16, 1890

Got up early, got the coffee on, Dannie cross, will he not try for
own sake to be a kind boy, I do pray for him that he may improve
in this, he will be a misery to us all if he keep on. He sat so sullen,
did not act right for 1 minute—he must take the horse, can I trust
him, I wrote Miss Miner a note to send by him, he is as if he was
studying mischief—I went to see if I can get what Mr. Huntington
owes me, no, nothing seems to be right this morning. This is one
of the bad weeks, it seems. I went to work for a Mrs. Hanke
down in a tent, she is to be confined. I can have her work but I
have to go to the ranche. I have for 2 weeks tried to go, what is it
that is holding me—I came home, Ollie must have been here, her
hat pin, dress &c are gone, what does it mean. I tried to sew,
wrote in this. Here comes the Horse Bally as I live, what is before
me.

June, Tuesday 17, 1890

I up so early, thinking of the one that now seems to fill my crave-
ings for a companion, will he be all to me—how I do seem to care
for John. God grant this may be a happy union. Worked all day to
get ready to start for the ranche, oh dear how I do dread this trip.
Can I ever get through with these worries. If I could have seen
John, I leave the childrens and my picture on the bible, he has the
key to my house & to my heart, how I seem to care for him, will
he be true, I seem to trust him since the 10. of June—I love as I
never thought I should. I had Dannie drive arround on the Boulevard to take Miss Miners Book to her, she paid me $4.00.

[June 18, 19, 20 blank]

June, Saturday 21, 1890

> Packed the goods, got them to the Elbert depot, Luis Cowdry
> helped us. Mrs Frick came and invited us

June, Sunday 22, 1890

> Started at 7, led Bally, so hot, got to Elizabeth at 12, had a cup of
> tea at Mrs. West's, fed Fanny & watered. Told [. . .] Got to Mrs.
> Rowleys at 5, he still alive, I got 13 lbs nice butter Got to
> Mrs. Nickolas at 11 at night, left Bally in the pasture, he so stiff,
> got Dannie, got home 1, had to break

June, Monday 23, 1890

> Was not able to work for anyone, so sunburned and exausted.
> Went to the Fort Worth Gen office to see about the RR paying for
> the colt, Rock Marie's colt, 1 year the 4th of May, killed by them
> on or about the 20th, worth to me $50.00. Will I ever get 5¢, I
> hope so. Went to the Freight Depot on Wyancoop & 19th, so hot.

June, Tuesday 24, 1890

> Went ½ day to Mrs. Cyphers, she such a sufferer & so good.

June, Wednesday 25, 1890

> Carried 7 lbs nice butter to Mrs Sorrells, let it go on what I owe
> her. Got Johns' *add* again, ½ day for her coarse shirts, easy work,
> she so glad to get the work, why could not I have had him in the
> beginning. I sent John a letter, he at Webster Mrs. Carpenter said.
> How I do hope he may get it. Went all of us to the dear prayer
> meeting, Ollie really affected for good. I got my envelopes for 6
> mo, 10¢ per week, now I can have a permanent seat. R Roe says
> come to get organ.

June, Thursday 26, 1890

> Got started early for Roe's storrage rooms, he telophoned the
> Freight office, no, the goods I shiped from Elbert are not started
> yet—we came as a guide for Roes single delivery, Jack as driver. I
> got a man in the row of 3 new bricks on 13 ave or Willow street
> to come and help us unload, a Mr Barnard, he lives in Wiers addi-

tion. Went to see Olive, wrote to John, got a stamp of a Mrs.
Sampson, opposite side from Anna on Welton 265. How I do want
to hear from John, my picture lay on the bible as I left it.

June, Friday 27, 1890

I sewed for Mrs Cyphers, she so good.

June, Saturday 28, 1890

Washed for myself, am so much hurried cannot find time to write
in this dear little book.

June, Sunday 29, 1890

Went to church

June, Monday 30, 1890

Washed for Mrs Cyphers

July, Tuesday 1, 1890

Took home some shirts for Mr Cyphers, this will pay all I owe
them. Fanny gave me some Egg's, butter & milk to help on my
preparations for the 4 of July.

July, Wednesday 2, 1890

Washed the few men's washings, Ollie doing all she can to earn,
we are so poor, can we ever do enough to get our bread—

July, Thursday 3, 1890

Ollie trying to bake some cake & bread so we will have something nice for our dinner. There is to be everything free, so the
papers state. I sent 1 more letter to John, why dont I hear one
word from him, he surely has a reason for this long silence, what
can it be. Must I be ever expecting truth and yet be so much dis-
appointed. If only *he* was here.

July, Friday 4, 1890

Up and dressed all & started for the parade on the streets of the
city of Denver at 8.30, a grand thing. We stood on our horse &
buggy on Broadway & 18 1 hour and watched the parade go by.
The Cable stoped to accomodate the people. We all had all the

lemonade we could use, saw old Frank J and Birt dog, I was at the Barbecue in Overland Park, Annis lost Olives red fan, we got a lot of bread & meat, 3 tin cups, went home, fed old Fanny, then to athletic park in the evening to the fireworks. Ollie sick, a bad Diareah, I had to get out of the buggy to go with her 2 different times on the way home. We see the Summit Fuel & feed Co on fire, Dan & Olive stopped off, we came on home so tired.

July, Saturday 5, 1890

Every thing needed clean, so we all worked buisy. I went over to help poor Mrs. Cypher's. She changed so, he dont like me, that is a sure thing. I have her kindest regard but not his.

July, Sunday 6, 1890

To church late, I cannot see why it must be so nearly every time.

July, Monday 7, 1890

Worked on Ollie's shally & pink & green check. Why don't I hear from my John, I am in earnest, can it be he is not, God forbid.

July, Tuesday 8, 1890

I sewed ¾ day for Mrs Cypher, so nervous I quit, came home with a bad headache. I cannot live so much longer, will he never send me one line, how anxious I am.

July, Wednesday 9, 1890

Went to Mrs. Corbins, got the staff of life, helped her all day 50¢. Olive baked for the picknick at Christal Lake, shall we go, it dont cost us a cent, yes. A letter from John at last, not one word of love or anything to seem he cares for me. He signs his name yours verry truly. I must, I will see what this means as sure as I shall live.

July, Thursday 10, 1890

We off on the 7:15 cable, all nice, did not let 1 see us, they only think we are spending our money, not so we have none to spend. A big crowd all so happy, Olive met Lundburg there, he is trying to get my dear girl. We home 6 ocl tired, he brought her, she dead in love with him, he as bad, will they be ever so. I fear but I must trust and wait. Someday I shall see what all this was for. I do pray god for her a better life than I have had.

July, Friday 11, 1890

Cleaned our house, fixed the border of the cealing, it looks nice.

July, Saturday 12, 1890

All so buisy to finish our dresses, mine has been 1 year on the way, I must finish it now. Dannie go[t?] his regular 5¢ scraps, then went in the hot sun to feed Fan, so hard he has went for 2 weeks nearly every day his ba

July, Sunday 13, 1890

Went not in the morn, Larkins had the buggy, did not get back till 11 ocl. He knew I did always go to Church. I had my black silk dress, Olive had her new Shallie, Lundburg he came at 5, she so nice in her new dress. I and Dan drove over to evening service. Anna Currier sat in my pew, she wants me to drive to the cemetary tomorrow, so I will or Tuesday. I will wash tomorrow, I must go out to work, that is sure.

July, Monday 14, 1890

Up early & washing, I have 3 mens work, so little. I washed all our clothes so Olive wont be bothered when I go, She hung out.

July, Tuesday 15, 1890

Washed & Ironed, cut Annas dress, went to Mrs Corbins, got bread. She acts like herself once more. They are a strange lot, the men. I owe $11.00 for milk, now I must go out to work.

July, Wednesday 16, 1890

Dannie and I & Olive to Prayer meeting, such a good meeting, she wanted to take a part, cannot find courage. She is so in love with the man Lundburg, she is earnest about everything, he is an honest man I do think. We stoped on the way to the Kikapoo Indian Medicine camp at the show on 13 & Larimer, has been there 3 weeks.

Dake

The Mountains in Summer

*When she left Denver, Emily had no intention of ending up at Dake.
She had been hired as cook for the Buffalo Creek Park Hotel by its
owner, J. A. Jamieson, who happened to be in the Van Hamm employment office in Denver when Emily was applying for work. She left that
very afternoon in her buggy, taking the old stage road into the mountains.
Buffalo Creek Park was a wide, pine-timbered mountain valley 42 miles
from Denver on the Denver and South Park Railway, with two trains a
day. The area had tiny cottages for rent, a grocery store, two lakes for
boating and fishing, and facilities for excursions. It was a popular resort,
but the hotel kitchen was more than Emily could cope with, and after one
day's work, she quit.*[45]

*She drove her buggy through Bailey, 50 miles northwest of Denver on
the north fork of the South Platte River, and on to Grant, population
100, a supply center for the mines at Slaughts, and the location of a summer resort hotel owned by D. N. Cassell. Mrs. Jane Jardine, the hotel
keeper, agreed to care for Emily's horse and buggy for the summer, and
Emily took the train to Webster, 3 miles above Grant.*[46]

*Webster, now gone, was a station on the Denver and South Park Rail-
way founded a dozen years earlier as a shipping point for the silver mines
in Hall's Valley to the west. Webster had charcoal kilns, boarding houses,
a saloon, and a general merchandise store kept by J. S. Chapman, whose
wife became Emily's friend. Emily spent a week working at Webster for
the stingy Mrs. Nethery before going to Dake, 5 miles farther up the railroad track.*[47]

The little town of Dake, 75 miles from Denver by rail, was at the peak of its prosperity and near the end of its short life when Emily worked there. It was located 2 miles below the top of Kenosha Pass in Park County, at an altitude of 10,200 feet. In 1890 Dake had a population of 200, twelve to fifteen charcoal kilns, a boarding house run by Mrs. Dake, a hotel owned by W. O'Brien, J. S. Chisholm's blacksmith shop, a horse dealer named Bill Walp, and a Pacific Express Company agent named Truman Ross. Alvin C. Dake had founded Dake in 1883 as one of his charcoal operations producing fuel for smelters (others were at Leadville, Colorado, and Maxwell, New Mexico). The kilns at Dake were managed by L. H. Dake, whose wife was Emily's kind employer. In another two years Dake would be a ghost town, abandoned along with many of Colorado's mines and smelters in the panic of 1893.[48]

July, Thursday 17, 1890

Went down with Dan to see if I cannot get a place in Denver to go out to work, tried every thing, 7 places, then the Employ offices, Mrs. Carls & Van Ham. A Mr. Jamieson there from Buffalo Park he hired me as Cook $35.00 month, can I stand it? My time commences to day, I am to drive out their 42 mi but I can make it, I am no cowward, God will keep me. It coming dusk & raining, the high precipices towering above me, Bear Creek running on the side. Suddenly I came out on a man feeding some calves. I am bad unwell, my clothes soaked. It is all right, I was welcomed & treated to the best, and a nice bed alone. The little bugs bothered.

July, Friday 18, 1890

She hath done what she could

On the road after a good night rest in Mrs. Eggleston spare bed, the little bed bugs made me get up. I washed out my cloths, I am bad in my periods these days—got started ½ 7, how I did want to get off at 6, they gave me their family group, a scene planting potatoes, 2. She knows all the Golden folks I used to be working for when Dannie was born in 1877. Such a strange life is mine. I got my buggy greased at the mountain nook, a nice place among the pines. Got Fanny shod at Evergreen, another Mountain town by Bear Creek, a nice Church where god shall be housed.

July, Saturday 19, 1890

>Got started from Mrs. Steels at ½ 7, no earlier, made it to the
chicken ranch all right, then over the big hill to Pine 2½ miles,
now to Buffalo Park. Got there at 10 ocl, so tired, Fanny & I
both. Now I must write to John & the dear folks at home, will
they do all right?

July, Sunday 20, 1890

>At the Buffalo Park Hotel as cook, Oh dear I shall die, 7 chickens,
15 lbs roast beef, 10 lbs veal, potatoes, beets, peas, Ice cream, currant pie &c, my first day with little help. Minnie the sweed girl
has a bad finger, she has poisoned it in a cut in her thumb, left
hand, I opened it, put poultice on. Boiled ham, cold roast for supper. So tired, must have breakfast at 6, can I make it?

July, Monday 21, 1890

>Up at 3 wrote in this dear little book. I am neglecting it so much
now for the work of the day. The fire is so dull, steak, mutton,
veal cutlets, I stood and fried till 8.30, it so tiresome. Can I stand
it? No, I could not find the oat meal, the coffee run out, Mrs.
Jamieson dont help me as she did Minnie. The sweed cook will
not have as much to worry him, they will have to furnish better.

July, Tuesday 22, 1890

>*Keep your selves in the love of God*
>Up early, 5, got the fire. As I was getting potatoes in the oven, in
came a man in white apron, he is the man we have been looking
for. I started in the buggy at 1.30, got to Mrs. Buen, 6, heard
there that Hardy only 2 miles, drove there, it dusk, her mother &
father & her brothers family there, a house full. I slept on the parlor floor.

July, Wednesday 23, 1890

>*Pray without ceasing*
>Slept oh so good last night on Mrs. Hardy's parlor floor, enjoyed
the converse, the morning the 19 Psalm, the prayer, such a home,
God so truly their guide. I thank him, he has kept me all these
years. This is my prayer, that his guiding care may be over me,

that I may ever do ought to bring a reproach on his dear name. 9
oclock I must start. I washed my handkerchief and neck ribbon,
Katie tried it on, I talked to Mrs. Bailey out in the yard, Mr B is
Mrs. Hardy's brother, she has them all arround her. Mr Hardy is
so poorly. The horse is fed, everything is nice. I shall long to see
them more, God bless them *all*. Fanny well, got to Grant 4 ocl,
Mrs. Surles keeps the store. She sent me to a Mrs. Jane Jardine,
Grant.

July, Thursday 24, 1890

Whosoever shall say to this mountain be thou removed

Mrs Jardine at Grant had breakfast for the men, coffee & potatoes,
salt meat, she seems to be a good woman. I cut and worked the
buttonholes on Miss Ellas satteen dress, hemmed the skirt, she is
telegraph operator at Webster, a good girl. Her sister was married
3 weeks ago, the mother feels her girl going so much—when can
I be home again? I am makeing nothing but my board, Oh heavenly father help me I do pray. I was talking of driving old Fanny
to Webster, Mrs. Chapman came from Denver last night, stoped
off here. I let them have the horse to drive over to Cassells, a
summer resort, so shady the grove. John Jardine was going up on
the train to Webster, I made up to go to leave Fanny to Mr Jardine, she gave my fare 20c. I came to Mrs Nethery to work for
my board, think of it, shall I ever get my debts paid at this rate,
washed all the P.M. hard, she is like all, get all the work she can.

July, Friday 25, 1890

Thou wilt show me the path of life

Up at Mrs Mary Nethery, a big washing come for Mrs. Chisholm
last night. Mrs. Jim Smith was here last night, her husband just
out of States Prison for killing his partner Grow, shot him down
with a shotgun. I tried to please the children, washed the dishes
&c, changed my clothes &c commenced at 9 to wash. They visiting all morning, they went to get gooseberries. I washing, got my
skirts & corset washed, all the same they so afraid one will have a
cent. Never mind, I must get home. I did not eat dinner with
them, the table is so little. I washed about 3. As I was working
Oh so hard, here come My John—Why do I love him so much? I

see something is not right, he wants to see me, I shall now be careful, I *must*. Can it be someone else has a claim on him? I can give him up but *oh dear*. Had Mrs. Netherly tell my fortune, she told it true, said I was to have trouble with a dark haired woman, yes, I had told Ella Jardine to bring Jenny tomorrow. Here is John

July, Saturday 26, 1890

There is a way that seemeth right to a man
I feel my days work yesterday, washing hard all day for an old woman is not the thing. She is cross as can be, but such is the way of life. We all feel our poverty. Pancakes & coffee and sour faces, but things will change. Mrs. Johnson, a light-haired neighbor, a sweed, came, brought a gray coat for repairs. Mrs. Nethery said I might have the job. I finished her job, then darned it so nice. took it to the man, a deaf sweed, he wanted a patch on, so the job was no good. Oh how I am troubled to earn a little money, will it ever be different, God be my helper. Mended and Ironed all the PM. Mr Nethery over in town trying to have his wife give up to live with him. She declares she will not unless he will stay sober. He is bound to try, so they made it up, the children so pleased. Nettie & I slept on the floor in the side room, she is 14, nice girl. We had boiled beef, potatoes &c. The men began coming for their washing, such a lot of them. She makes lots of money.

July, Sunday 27, 1890

Thou has guided me with strength
I got up, built the fire, tucked the ticking skirt she gave me. I found 4 pins points toward me, now see if John will come—we had griddle cakes & coffee, syrup for breakfast. Mr Nethery here the first time, he is nice looking man if he can only resist that awful habit. I pray earnestly for them. She told my fortune with the cards, I am to earn some money & get it, be sorely disapointed. Just now as I am writing, 2.15, the watch gave a twir and stoped, more expense. I have so much to trouble me, are they all well at home? The bread is light. I must make the fire. Mrs. N is in the school house next door writing. Such a lonesome day, I went out on the Bank of the Platte and sat me down, how I do want to see the children—

July, Monday 28, 1890

> *Give thanks. Who is like unto thee O lord*
> Up & got the fire built for Nettie, she so sleepy. Mrs Netherly
> cross as usual. I got ready to go to a Mrs Chapman's to wash—
> she concluded to have a wine col. cashmere made over for a
> morning dress. She laid $5.00 on the machine to send to Mr
> Longfellow, now no lien can be on our house. I wrote to Ollie &
> Dan.

July, Tuesday 29, 1890

> Sent Halleck & Howard $4.00, Mrs Nethery lent me 10¢, now I
> feel as if I should be able to weather the storm. I should like to see
> John but he seems to act so queer

July, Wednesday 30, 1890

> Washed for Mrs Chapman, she went down to her husbands store,
> got a letter from the children, the verry first I have had. I left
> home of the 17th, 18 Ollie's birthday without mother. I knew
> they had little, I sent $1.00, how kind of Mrs Corbin.

July, Thursday 31, 1890

> *He that cometh to me I will in no wise cast out*
> Nettie got up near morning & sat on me. The slats all went down
> and the bed through the floor. She danced all night last night and
> they are all of them bad off. I got up at 5, lit the fire. It rained
> hard all yesterday afternoon & night so the wood is wet. I took
> my shoes to Mrs Johnson's, her husband has the management of
> the shoe shop. I got some yeast for Mrs Nevery, all asleep. I got
> back, commenced breakfast, got the boiler on. Nevery got up,
> brought a tub full. We eat breakfast, Pancakes & coffee, then I
> went at the washing. Mrs. Hathaways & Mrs. Carrolls, she D. C.
> Bailups sister. I am getting to find a few that know me. I don't see
> John someway. I got my shoes and warmed a cup of tea, hurried
> for the train to Dake. I am to go there to work. What then, shall I
> succeed—

August, Friday 1, 1890

> *The Lord is verry compasionate & pityful*

Up early, breakfast with Mr & Mrs Dake & the little girls, Cora 20 mo, Fernie 3 years on June 8th—she is going to see if I cannot get the boys kiln clothes, they think I may do well. Mrs. Kelly & Dake went to see Mrs Chisholm if she would see the boys about it. She came to see me—I washed for Mrs. Dake, 2 doub 2 single blankets, a pail full of Didas &c. Mrs. Conklin & Donoho came here to sew, I did not want to visit with them, sat down after I was done in the shed, finally had to come in, combed my hair, changed to my casemer, sat with them a while, they went. Mrs. Dake got supper, buiscuit, cake, potatoes, corn, canned peaches, tea, nice, butter, cream cheese, good. I sat down & wrote to Mrs Corbin, told her that a Mrs Pettis was to go to see the children for me. It is raining hard. Mr Dake is not feeling well—
[on front flyleaf]: Aug 1   Sitting by Mrs. Dake's light, so far from home tonight

August, Saturday 2, 1890

I have trodden the wine press alone

Mrs. Dake got Bill Walp washing, I put on the water, I had it near done when Earnest Kinkear came, he brought 5 pieces. Now though it is Saturday I hope I may do well. I wrote a line to Mrs Chapman, told them to get me a box of soap. She gave me a nice apron, a pair of stockings, a lovely bed, I had a book & rocking chair, I enjoyed it so much. I must not fail to mention my going down to see about old Fanny, she is all safe at Mr Jardines. Mrs Carroll & Mabel here at Grant. I started on foot for Webster, got there at 5, such a kind reception, how can I ever repay them, she jokering so much. Mrs. Carroll came, she not so pleasant a woman but such must be let to pass. Minnie Nethery playing in the oats they tore Mabells hat, a row. I was tired nearly out walking from Grant.

August, Sunday 3, 1890

Them that honor me I will honour

Up & reading the Bible, Granny rattleing her stove in the next room. I had a Volume Haskells Poems she handed me, nice. I combed my hair, went out with the kit, she gave me her Bible, how good, also a box of pills—I ate ginger cake & drank tea.

While yet eating Mrs Carroll came, she did not like my telling
about her Brothers act. He mortgaged his ranche to a Mrs Kracaw
& let her take it a sly way of getting all or more than it was
worth. I never meant to make her feel bad. D. C. Barley never did
me any harm, I do want to be friends. John he dont like Chis-
holms, sat on the Depot platform, I had a long talk with him, he
is going to get Dannie here. I sent for my trunk. I came up to
Dake, sent a line to him, here all stared. Cant I write to John—

August, Monday 4, 1890

He took me, He drew me out of many waters

Not feeling so well as I wish, yet I got the breakfast. He praised
the coffee. She up in time for her griddle cakes, they good, Maple
Syrup. Now for washing a big one. I am rubbing all the clothes,
she puts them to boil, a square lard can all she has. I have the stable of them, he is mudding up the logs, kind of them. I can get
the old stove of Shorty, he says (he is only 6 foot-5, a tall man, his
name Roberson, he is swell on Annie O'Brien, they say. They
have 6 boarders & work both of them hard. We all had the lines
full at 2. It rained, we had to take our starch clothes in. I sat down
first at 5, worked 6 buttonholes on Mrs Chapmans dress I have
cut & made so far, I must finish it. Am I soon to close this life,
will be better.

August, Tuesday 5, 1890

They will be done, Dear Lord

Mrs Dake set the alarm 5 oclock, it went off, she put it under the
quilt so it would not disturb me. She got up, went to her Ironing.
I got up at 6, got a small table in that was outside the house, put a
sack and a pillow tick on it, went to helping her. She not well, so
ambitious. I surprised by Godfrey Ragle, a German, he came with
4 white shirts, 4 towels, 3 wool so dirty. I found 3 good blankets,
she will let me use them if I wash them, so I will and Cora's
cloths. I wrote a word to Olive & Dan, told them to send my
trunk when John Lawson cam back. He will stay in the mines
even if I give him up. Mrs. Dake wrote a nice letter to my Dear
Olive, bless her, how brave she is all alone, will I soon earn so I
can send to them, God can let this end and me rest, I do trust.

Mrs OBrien came in for a little talk she is getting large I may not wait, soaked her feet.

August, Wednesday 6, 1890

God will supply all our needs

I got up & lit a fire, cooked oatmeal, made coffee, griddle cakes. He feels clever towards me. She dont feel like getting up, I made her a piece of toast, she dizzy. I combed my hair, starched the white shirts 4, went to Ironing them—she roasted a beef heart with dressing, so nice. I done the dishes, she feels so bad, then I went at the mending, 9 shirts, 4 towels, 2 collars, he got them at evening, gave me $1.25 for them, good. A man, Joe Mayer, brought 3 shirts this morning for me to wash. I cut my finger, will I get enough to do? I feel lonely to night, will this be so long, I do so crave love, this dear woman does love one, I believe. Mr. J. H. McLain the photograh, brought his washing. I did dream of John last night, he met me on the stairs. I cannot, must not forget this dream, how I talked & planned on the stairs.

August, Thursday 7, 1890

What think ye of Christ

Mr Dake up at midnight to go and take Mr Jerry Kelley place at the kilns, he not well. The swamp in front of the houses is so verry unhealthy, Mrs. Dake sick all day yesterday. I have the Photographers wash, Godfrey Ragle going to give me one of his pictures. We cleaned out the place I am going to live in, the bedstead I am to have, the Priest has used in the old Boarding house. He came 2d to minister to the people, this is right. Mrs Kelley wants me to go and stay at her home, she is alone tonight—I have to get on the clothes, they are dry, look good. The children, Ferny & Cora & Reddy the dog, went for their pictures. I do hope they will be nice ones. I changed my dress, I wrote to dear John, will I hear soon? oh how lonely is my life to me, I deserve better things.

August, Friday 8, 1890

He was a man of sorrow and acquainted with grief

Got up at Kelly's at 7, she a nice woman, griddle cakes & tea rolls. I went to Dakes back door, fastened, went to the window, Cora

cried—Fenchen Fenchen, her name for me. She had her dishes
washed, we went up to get Ross washing, not till Monday. We
got three roses to put in the house I am to live in. I starched the 3
collars, 3 shirts for the Photographer F. S. McLean. I commenced
to iron them, had a bad spell with my heart, could scarcely
breath. Got my corset off, felt no better, my eye lid puffed up like
glass. So queer, I so sick all day, I can get no rest, the children
keep such a din. There is no rest where a child is. Must I never
have rest, I am thinking not, & I mended till dark, then went up
to Kelley to stay all night, she so glad. Willie & she not well, I
was sick near all night, she so kind.

August, Saturday 9, 1890

Got up at 7.30. I feel better but oh how I miss my home. I stay
with Dake through the day, I eat break Kelley, oatmeal, tea, griddle cakes, peach pie. She gave me a lace flower for a birthday gift.
I have an embroider apron from Mrs. Chapman, she so good. I
came to Mrs Dake's, she buisy with her bakeing, I went to my
mending. She so pleasant & chatty. I cleaned up the children,
swept the dining room and kitchen. We had stew, Raspberry pie,
such cream, Potatoes in milk, tea. I must be so ungrateful if I do
not recognize Gods hand in this, he is surely helping, yet the devil
is ready to pervert everything and do all he can to make me enemies—Mrs. Dake went with $2.00 of my hard earnings to get
me an express order from Kenosha, 2 miles above here, Dake. I
got a letter from Olive dear, she needs a pair of shoes so bad.

August, Sunday 10, 1890

Whoso putteth his trust in the lord they shall be safe—Amen
We lay in bed till 9 oclock—no need of our getting up early. We
talked a long time. I got up, fire wont burn, had to get kindling,
twice cooked oatmeal &c, we enjoyed our breakfast—Bill Walp he
came by cursing as usual, he knows no God, no Sunday, poor
soul. I went to Mrs. Dakes, changed my dress, sat down to read a
story, the flies just awful, lay down, no sleep—I went into Mrs.
OBrien, no one arround. I made the fire, Johnnie O.B. came, they
have the Boarding house, he set the table. I went to Dakes, she
had currant bread, lemon pie.

August, Monday 11, 1890

Mrs. Kelley lay with Willie, he a sick boy. I went over to Dakes, she going to help me wash today. I got the water on, had to bring it from the spring. A hard rain last night, the swamp muddy

August, Tuesday 12, 1890

Not by night nor by power but by my spirit saith the lord of hosts
I got up early at Kelleys to wash for her. I went to Mrs. Donoho's to get some calicoes, then washed a quilt for Kelleys. That lovely little woman Mrs Chapman came up on the train, Mr. A. C. Dake also. Dr. Bradley & wife in their buggy from Beuna Vista Col, she has just lost her baby, 5 weeks old.

August, Wednesday 13, 1890

We up late, it raining all night, the fire wont burn. I tried to get one while she went to get milk. Mr. A. C. Dake came to pay her the wages, her husband earned $86.00. How I wish I had some one to get for me, no, I can earn for myself. Mrs. Kelley paid me 75¢, so kind. Willie just had a good movement of the bowells, now he will sleep. I went to Chisholms for the Ver, worms is troubling him—

August, Thursday 14, 1890

The lord pitieth those that fear him, he knoweth our frames
Got up at 6, left Mrs. Kelley and Willie sleeping. She cried half the night, poor woman, her husband away at Leadville being treated lumbago—she paid me 75¢ for a little washing. He came home today, looks so terrible bad. I come to Mrs Dakes to stay with her children while she went with Dr and Mrs Bradley to pick berries, if they only get a few. I got dinner on time, what a nice time I would have if I only had a home and some one that was as they ought to be to furnish it. It is my birthday, 2 nice aprons I washed for Mrs Dr Bradly, she paid me $1.00, 2 white skirts, 10 b.d., 1 apron, cloths unwell. Shorty gave me some clothes, coal dirty, for Dannie, I washed them. Mrs Dake came at 6, no berries, they had mushrooms, so good. They so happy both, how nice. 9 nice boiled out flour sacks from Mrs O Brien, nice.

August, Friday 15, 1890

I slept with Cora & Ferny Dake in the bedroom, could not get to
sleep, no use, got up, lay down on the carpet, no use, they are
making so much noise in the next house, Dr Bradley & Bill,
whiskey makes them jolly & noisy. I got to sleep, just at morning
dreamed of Mr Lawson, he was feeding stock & pigs. Mrs. Cowdry gave me a large gold hunting case, gold watch, verry nice,
said I was worthy. After breadfast at Dakes, cake & coffee and
peaches & such cream, I went to Mrs Kellys to sew on Mrs Chapmans dress, got the skirt all hemmed and gaged. Mrs. Kelley got a
teakettle. At noon when the train came in from Denver there was
Dan on & three letters from Ollie & sister, in one a hankerchief
with "mother" worked in her hair, she is so loveing to poor
mother. I went and whipped cream for Dake, she getting a supper
for Dr Bradleys, they have a nice lot of mushrooms. I slept again
with her children, he so good now to her.

August, Saturday 16, 1890

God bless & keep my boy here from all harm, for his own name sake
Amen
I up at 5, built Mrs Dakes fire, put on her breakfast to cook, then
went to write some letters to sister & Olive. She had written a
long begging letter concerning Mr Lawson, no, I must not be
foolish. He is not the man I could be a happy woman with, I
thought so once, I do not now. Dannie says Mr A. C. Dake gave
Olive a $1.00 or more, I dont think he did. Wayne Tomlinson
must have been in good buisiness disturbing Ollie. I finished Mrs
Chapmans dress in the stable I am to live in. I helped the girls,
Annie O, Ray Dake, & Bradley, to get off in the Dr Buggy to
Webster to carry this Dress home and get the views of the camp. I
baked her bread, Ironed some, washed the window in the house,
got the church ready for Dannie to do. She is nearly out of butter,
uses it so free. I was at work, Mr OBrien sent A in for me. Now
for buisiness for me. Dannie went alone to bed, so good.

August, Sunday 17, 1890

Such a long hard night with Mrs OBrien, her labor so protracted.
Dr Bradley a nice man & a No 1 physician, he so careful of her.

The labour slow, she 30 past, no wonder she has a hard time. It is her first child, it had to be born on the floor, he did not want to use instruments. It such a nice plump thing, but cried while being dressed. She wanted it christened Marguirett Agnes. I dressed it in its christening robes, verry nice & sent to it from N Jersey. The Priest here in Dake held Mass, Rev. Father Wortner, then came to the Boarding house, Mr O B keeps it, he christened the baby. Mr & Mrs Chisholm were its god father & mother. I never saw Dannie till 3 this P.M., he wandering all over camp. Harry Clay came back to camp and brought his bride and a jug of Rye Whiskey, too bad. I am now employed steady.

August, Monday 18, 1890

Fear not they that are able to kill the body But rather fear ye the Lord
Up 5, slept with Miss Anna O. B. I rested so good all night—The Dr in, he looks rested. We had a hard night saturday night from 5 till morning, now she is so comfortable with her sweet baby—I fixed baby, fed her, then I cleaned the mothers bed—put all clean clothes on her & the bed, she looks so nice. Mrs Kelley came, they treat all to cake, fruit & wine. This child is a god send to them both, oh why could not I have had such a home—I cut out my calico dress that dear Olive has sent to me by Daniel. I washed all the clothes through twice, ready for tomorrow—Charley McArthur came, he the man that told me he was sure I would do well up here. He took Mrs. Jardines glasses home, he her soninlaw. Such a night, baby wont nurse, oh dear. Myres paid 50¢, Dannie helping Dake good all day. I lay down on the floor dressed, 2^{00}. Mr O B so cross—

August, Tuesday 19, 1890

I up just as breakfast ready, the Iron piece they rap on such a heavy noise. I have my hands full to please so many, but god is able to help me, I am trying so hard to please. I took oil as I got up and kneeded her breasts, she wont help to get the baby to nurse one bit, he gave it some whiskey last night all the same, to-day I have not seen one happy moment. Either the Dr has been cited by some old woman or else I could not do as someone else did. Certainly I am either a fool or else the devil must be a sure

enemy of mine. I will yet hope and pray, for I am so dull and near
sick, can I recover my spirit after such treatment? Dake feels it yet
more than I do, she bought & brought in a good baby pin, she is
so kind, they just impose on her. Mrs Bradley came in, she is such
a dear little woman, so good. Ferny got knife & spoon. I took a
cathartic pill tonight, I am over my unwell time a day.

August, Wednesday 20, 1890

I looked for some to take pity but there was none to comfort
but I found none

I feel to sick to rise but must—she not so cross as last night but
cross enough. Now again I will try what I can do to please—I
fixed the fire, carried out the slops, then fixed her breakfast—beef
broth, bread, tea &c, my own tea, potatoes, Doughnuts. They
going to scrub, Jake Larson late to his, he sick. I put the clothes
into a clean water. It rained hard all night, the ditch washed out,
we shall have to wait till it is repaired. I cleaned the potatoes, then
my hair I gave a good one combing, I washed the dishes for
Anna, she so thankful. She made cake, Dr Bradley & wife came
he in, he gave Mrs OBrien an injection, she so queer, I am glad he
will. I received a good letter from Mrs. Corbin, she so nice, I
wrote to Ollie & Corbin, I got a picture of the kilns for Corbin,
$1.00, she is so good I cannot do enough, she has been so good to
me.

August, Thursday 21, 1890

I up most of the night, Baby has a colic, I think, I pray she may
do well, she is such a sweet little thing, she dont get enough milk
from her mother but she is learning to nurse all right. I dressed
her, her mother does make me so nervous fussing at me so much.
I put the greased cloth in my pocket so I can show it if she says
anything. I ought to be let fix it. They all seem to boss me. Last
night both got up and left me in bed, I did not dare get up for
they talk so mean to me. I commenced to wash at 9, such a big
wash, I am to do it alone. I see she dont care for me, not one bit,
not a kind word or look, how long can I stand this? I must try for
yet a while. What am I to do, this is so strange, has she no heart,
some women have not—god will help me. She had Dr look at the
naval, he said I had it all right, now she must find something else.

August, Friday 22, 1890
> *They word is a lamp unto my feet and a light unto my path* amen

Baby cried all night. For all of the fuss I got up at 5, emptied the
slops, that seems all I am to be allowed to do. Another Mrs
Georgia for all the world, stingy as she was. She dressed &
washed her baby herself today. She did not like it because I did
not strip the baby off, I wish I had. The Drs wife is going to do it
tomorrow. I sent Olive's picture of Dake, also Mrs. Corbin 1 of
the Kilns—Ironed all day, washed the Dishes 3 times, Anna seems
to like me or my help, one. I fitted my dress on in her room, it
fits nice. I can make a dress *sure*. As I went to my dress I found I
was come unwell, from the 19th till now over time. I had such a
pain by my heart all P.M., went to bed so tired. I sewed about ½
hour on Dakes Singer on Dannie's shirt.

August, Saturday 23, 1890
> Got up when Anna did, only brushed my hair, went straight and
had a talk with her. She don't want me after tonight, she is going
to make Anna be her nurse. I can do her washing. I was so careful
not to say one thing to anger her, now shall we see what a fair lot
they are. I shall not earn verry much at this job, sure. I must again
go to the washing. The Dr & wife going today, sorry, she is a
sweet little woman, they are not to be blamed for what she is
doing. She treats me better today, I will always treat everyone
fair. I choped the raisines, beat the frosting, whipped the cream,
made a peach pie, helped with everything. He paid me $10.50. At
evening I saw Ross, gave it to him to get me an express order at
Kenosha to send to Ollie, she can pay some bills for me. The child
has not written to me for 1 week, why is it? I made Dannie a shirt
after 6 so he might be a clean boy tomorrow.

August, Sunday 24, 1890
> *The soul of the diligent shall be made fat*

I did not get up when Anna did, she does not feel well, that is
sure. I stirred the bed &c. Now I am paid, I have to get something
else to do, will it pay me. I went up to the house and laid down,
had my breakfast, helped wash the dishes, Johnny so funny. She
dont allow me to touch the baby, she is a verry strange selfish
woman. I am going to do their washing tomorrow, then I must

see what I can get besides. God do send me work that will make
me some money. This has been a failure in part, if she had not had
a Dr she would have conniptioned sure. I ought to be thankful I
have escaped so easy—Dannie tries to help Mrs Dake all he can,
he seems to be all right with me.

August, Monday 25, 1890

I will bless the lord at all times Amen

I up early, combed my hair good, eat my breakfast, carried her a
cup of coffee, she looks so ugly at me. This is the last, I never suffered more in nursing a sick woman. She is an Irish Catholic, need
I try to please, had I come here dressed and soft hands I might
barely have pleased but I am a hard worked woman, that is all. I
went at the washing, am to get 25¢ a doz, think of that. I cant
earn my salt, groceries are so dear, $3½ a lb for Potatoes, flour 4¢,
butter 50¢, meat 16¢. I got done at 1.30, had 4½ doz pieces, such
a nice mess from the bed, she must be crazy to ask me to do such
a wash for such a price. I went and done what I could to fix my
little cabin. There I must now try to live. Godrey Kinear & Robertson all have some washing, also W. Walp.

August, Tuesday 26, 1890

I have learned whatever my lot to be content

I must get up and get things ready to do Mrs Dake's wash, she is
realy sick. I can do Godfreys in with her's so I will not be so
crowded at the last. She put her clothes soaking over night, so
good. I got her clothes out, then went at the Blanket & the others,
8 shirts, 3 pair drawers, 5 towels, oh so black. I got done 5.30, so
tired. Dannie helps good.

August, Wednesday 27, 1890

Rise and pray lest ye enter into temptation

Mrs Dake calls me to come and get breakfast. I took the ground
coffee down, asked him if I might leave it. I did not use it and it
would only go to waste, he did not care so I left it. I got his br.
Mr Truman Ross, sent me a nice lot of work, I do pray I may do
enough to live. I washed 1 fine casimere shirt, 1 beadspread, pillow cases, handkerchiefs, 1 black silk, his overcoat &c. Dress suit

to clean pants & fix the bottoms. I did all for 75¢, too cheap but I must.

August, Thursday 28, 1890

Happy is everyone that findeth wisdom

Must get up and hurry—I hear her call. I can get her breakfast for her good, I never shall contentedly eat idle bread. Dannie must do her churning, then he pays a lot of his board—I washed all the morning Mr Robersons Kiln clothes, so dirty, three suits, Stowells he wants them mended—a double blanket, 2 shirts, 1 towell for Kinear. I got them out, then sewed till it was time to get our supper—how long shall I be able to stand this life? tis so hard, yet Mrs Dake, the dear sweet little woman, tries so hard to make me at home. She will never know how much I realy appreciate this all, I fear. I sometime may be able to let her see it all as I realy mean.

August, Friday 29, 1890

I will lay me down in peace to sleep

Can I do all I have to today? cleaned her windows, washed the shelf, lambrequin and window cloth, cleaned the dining room so nice. I washed and starched Eva's skirt the 3rd time, washed Ross Black silk handkerchief, had a big hunt for it, found it under the gutter pipe where the wind had blown it, a big dust whirlwind came and fixed things for us—washed a spread, shirt, cases & towel & mended Ross Pants so nice, he must be pleased with them—cleaned his fine suit with Benzine. Mrs Dake came up to our cabin, invited us down to eat mellon. I took Dannie's pants I am trying to make over. Frank Cole gave him 2 pairs, one is so fine casimere. I washed the cotton. Does seem sometimes as if Mr Dake is sorry he is so verry strange, but he is so bad. She feels bad, caught cold, stoppage. I fixed to soak her feet, she took 4 hour doses Ergot, her menses started again good—

August, Saturday 30, 1890

Great is the mystery of godliness, Amen

I so verry tired I dont feel as if could get up. I have all the mens washing to patch, how I wish Olive would write to me, it is 2

weeks and a day to day, not 1 word from her. What can it mean. I
fixed Eva D's skirt, fluted it by hand—It looked so nice she paid
me 25¢. I put all in their seperate bundles so their will be no confusion when they come for them. I finished my gown commenced
2 weeks ago—then sewed on the cuffs of Wm Walps shirt, it has
shrunk so tis scarce large enough for my boy—the mail came, no
letter. Oh dear me. I went to Mrs Dake to bake her bread while
she went to see Mrs Donohoe. I was invited but I must work. Eva
& her husband are going to Webster to the Dance. Mr Dake has
gone to Halls Valley to the Picnic, they all go to Webster this eve.
A new black calico Olive sent, and Mrs Dake & her children did
not come till 10.30. I sat, sewed on her singer machine, got my
dress done.

August, Sunday 31, 1890

Be ye steadfast always abounding in good work
I Sneezed today, look out. I waked up hearing Mr Dake & Bill
talking about the betting at the PicNic, $20.00, Bill lost. He said
he had a big Brown taste in his mouth, how bad to abuse themselves. Dannie made a fire, we had some warmed potatoes, a little
cold bread pudding, some new bread, tea. She gave Dannie some
coffee, he done up her Dishes, then changed his clothes, I put on
my cashemer. I must be disapointed and yet I do hope either
Olive will come or else send a letter. I combed Mrs Dake's hair,
cut out a nice piece to make hair flowers, tis so long, just like my
dear Ollie's. The mail has come, oh nothing for me. Godfrey got
his clothes, did not pay. I ventured into Mrs OBs, held the baby
10 minutes, went into see her, she looks pale but the old look is in
her eye. I came here in this little lonely bare ground cabin to sit
and write in this dear & only friend I seem to have, it will never
go back on me. Dan just came, asked to go to Donohoe's for 1
hour, yes. Baked on her stove yesterday—

September, Monday 1, 1890

If we suffer we shall also be with him
Mrs OBrien sent last night for me to wash, then Dr said it would
not be for the best. I had to give in. Mrs Dake had me to help her,
I washed then 2 white shirts, 2 collars for Godfrey Ragle, had all

done 4, sewed some for Daniel, must fix his clothes so he can
soon go to school, fixed his drawers, he had none when he come,
no undershirt, only the one on him, graybacks on that. I must fix
a colored shirt she has given me for him—the surveyors for the
new road came for dinner. Mrs Dake got $3.50 for the 7 men. We
worked hard, made 2 pies, fried steak. I sewed till the 1 oclock
train in the morning went down.

September, Tuesday 2, 1890

He maketh me to lie down in green pastures
I was tired to get up, could not eat, went to the work, it rained towards morning, cannot wash the water in the tubs that runs from
the swamps, always so riley after a rain. I shall iron. I got the
white shirts so nice, also my other clothes. I do need to be so patient—such a gossipy little hole, I shall soon leave it—I got 3 postal cards today from Ollie & sister. If they had only sent them
before I sent the special delivery yesterday to Mrs. Corbin and a
letter to Mr Ed Lundburg. Ollie says he is verry sick, how bad, it
is sure I must go home soon. Ann O. B. and Kelley done all the
baby clothes, so I loose 2 doz. pieces, all so kind, you know.

September, Wednesday 3, 1890

The serpent beguiled Eve—
Anna O. Brien told me to come and wash so I will go, shall do it
out of doors, then the noise cannot hurt her. They try to blame
every one all they can, she is so verry ugly, treats Mrs D as hateful
as she does me. An old Mexican woman came along with honey,
Butter, Eggs, chickens & string beans &c, they all got of her 50¢
for chickens half grown, 30¢ for eggs, so dear I cannot get—the
surveyors cook came 8, E. Newell, with washing. They are clean
& nice, I put them soaking, will do them this P.M. She is cross
about it, dont want me to get anything to do. Ross is getting up a
party, sent Dan 7 miles to Case. I washed & ironed the clothes for
Newell, he can get them in the morning, 85¢.

September, Thursday 4, 1890

What I do thou shalt know hereafter
2 oclock when we got home. I went to Dakes house 4 times last

night to see the little ones, once I found Cora up crying for a drink—I gave it, she lay down so good. I saw a Miss Tutsdale, Rosses new girl. He has mashed on every one around. This is Mrs Case's sister, twas to her that Dannie had to go to see if they were coming, yes. They are nice, all of them, 5 women, 4 men, all so smart, the violin player, the whole party. Good whiskey, nearly kept out a little from an old bottle at Lymands. She hates it, but what is a poor woman to do. Have not I had to go through all this. I mended and done at her churning, she could sew, she run around all day, got cross and said a few cross words, the first

September, Friday 5, 1890

The fountain of living water's

Wrote to Dear Mrs Chapman. I up and in the early cold fixing Dannie's pants. He does tear his clothes so. Dakes seem so strange to me since the Dance at the Store. Ross & he got it up, she invited us. I was so lonesome I went and looked on only, I said not 1 word to anyone, had to speak to old Mrs. Chisholm, she is perfect—old Mrs. Whiting says no good word for any one. I feel so bad tonight—Kelley hardly spoke to me. I will go home soon. I sewed on some pants and a blouse for Dan, he runs away so. It is midnight, I am sitting here, Dan asleep. So cold writing, sneezed 2 or 3 times to day—I am on the point of going home, oh dear &c, 7 &c sent their recept, they have not put the $4.00 on the note, *all bad*. Mrs Dake came, paid me for the sack flour, $1.00 coffee, 25¢, so kind of her. I shall go soon.

September, Saturday 6, 1890

Watchman what of the night

I must get up, and after my poor breakfast go to Mrs Dake mending so many of her children aprons. I brought 7 up, hung on the partition slats, just room for Robertsons old stove, he has given it to me, no top, no leg, such an old concern. I am glad to get it nevertheless. Mrs. O.B. is going to send her washing to Mrs Nethery, see how mean they act. Minnie Nethery came today, I made over a knit jacket for Dan, got his pant done, the ones that Frank Cole gave. Finished my calico Dress, have all the old mending done. On the train came Mrs Pettis and a Mrs Huston and 2

little girls. I have known they were comeing several days. She did
not want anybody to know, they are so mean. I staid all day
alone, Dan read out to me while I worked. It is so cold, Oh dear,
must go.

September, Sunday 7, 1890

I am poor & needy! the lord pitieth me

I lay long dreading to get up, nothing in life for us. Godfrey paid
me $1.00, Kiner 95, Joe Myers $1.00, Robertson $1.25. I read af-
ter I had got my poor work done, such a long lonesome day.
Dannie went to the lake, I could not stand it to go—here goes old
Mrs. Chisholm, an Irish bitch, another Mrs Whiting. If I had lots
of money I would be all right. I put Mrs Dakes clothes to soak. I
am going to do hers, then go home. I wrote to Mrs Jardine to find
out if Fanny is all right, to Ollie she can expect me.

September, Monday 8, 1890

Christ the first fruit! corn die

I up at 5 and went to work washing. Kiner sent his, Frank Cole
came, brought a big bundle. I began to pick up, got the first out
on the line 9 oclock, all done & ironing at 3, she will be glad.
Packed and fixed till 1 A.M., am writing now, so tired I can
scarcely see the lines. Will start for Home in the morning or in a
few short hours, what a long hard trip for me.

September, Tuesday 9, 1890

My feet slipeth, hold me up Lord

This is the last day at Dake. I can see strange actions. I hear she
was so for Ferny before he married her. I cleaned up the stable I
have lived in. She dont come much, why, who is to blame? I
could not get a freight, they are haveing so much trouble running
off the track. She gave me 50¢ for the washing—She has given me
everything to live on. I got all my things, bid her good bye. Ferny
is sick, so is Cora. I got a ride with Case the meat man of South
Park, got in Webster at 7 ocl to see Mrs Nethery, got my ticket.
Mr Grant saw Mr Chapman, he would not take anything for the
soap. He got my dinner at the Hotel, we went to the house got

my bundle, he so kind on the train. I got to Mrs Jardines 3, sprin-
kled & Ironed lots, lent her $7.50 to pay express on groceries.

September, Wednesday 10, 1890
My steps had well nigh sliped
Heard Mrs Jardine setting the table, must get up 6 ocl. The men
all out feeding, haul wood all the time. Jardine has a contract with
some firm in Denver to send car loads of wood. I told her I would
do the work if she would go to her daughter Jennie McArthur.
Danny can drive. She had Bread to bake, did not want to leave
me so much to do. I went to work. She finally said she would go,
she made all the beds, put her plants in the buggy. I had Dan put
on a white shirt, he can be nice. Charly Rose come from Sleights
at daylight, eat breakfast with us. I baked a cake, got the dinner,
boiled potatoes, stewed veal, Bread, Prune Pie, tea, coffee, cu-
cumbers. I cleaned the windows, made 11 loaves of bread, washed
a pair of overalls for my Dannie, got supper, fixed for breakfast.

September, Thursday 11, 1890
Let us not be weary in welldoing
Mr Jardine called 5.30, I got up, dressed and out in 10 minutes.
Had the Breakfast before they did at the section house over the
way & cleaned 7 windows, made apple pies 3, so will have
enough for tomorrow, had a good vegetable soup. Old Mrs. Sny-
der, an old rip, came here, I left the house, she is a terror, was after butter, he got her some. I got a chance to sit down a while, I
am tired. But it is a change from a life in a small low cow house.
Got supper, had to wait till 7.30 for Harry Smith to come, he got
a big load, the roads bad. I worked the buttonholes in my sack
night dress, wrote in this little book. Charly McArthur, Charly
Rose here today. I am sure I saw A C Dake on the train this afternoon—It is time he went to pay off.

September, Friday 12, 1890
Cast thy burden on the Lord
I am so sleepy this morning, but Harry has made the fire and has
rapped on the wall, now I must rise and get the breakfast for
them—done, now I must bake a cake & some pies 3. I boiled

some ham bones & some potatoes & cabbage, she came at noon. I
done the work, she had a chill & some fever bad. His check came
to day. He paid me the $7.50 I lent her on Tuesday night while I
was ironing. Now I can go & have done good to a friend.

September, Saturday 13, 1890

   The lord is my shepard! I should not want he leadeth me—
I never awoke till 6, heard her setting the table—I had Dan run
the buggy up in front of the porch where I landed in July so discouraged—now I am going home, God help me to so be thankful
to him for all his benefits. We put all into the buggy. She gave me
potatoes, meat &c, she is near sick this cold morning. She has the
chance to go again to her daughters, Mrs Jennie McArthurs—I
started 8³⁰. Fanny shod all round, can travel good now. We got to
Charly McArthurs 10.00, she gave me a bottle of milk, I would
not get out for dinner, fed & eat our lunch at the bridge crosses
the Platte near Bailey, put dirt on the plants. Head aches, Mrs
Seely has had a drunken experience similar to mine, was robbed
and left to beg or starve, a Christian man came. I got this heading
from the lady, the one I asked to

September, Sunday 14, 1890

   Lay awake since midnight—talking with Mrs Seely, she came
from Maine, was a Mrs Richerdson, has 4 sons now all doing
well, 2 hire on a ranch near her, they came to stay with her all
night—I got there just at dark, she said I could stay in welcome.
We put Fanny in a little shed, fed her the grain Mr Jardine gave us.
In the morning the boy's went & brought some hay in sack's. I
cooked some of the meat for the Boys, they seem to be a different
lot. We started 7.30, got to Bradford Junction 9, took the Turkey
creek road, the last part so high & narrow sloped, and inquired of
Mrs Nellie Rambo. Hutchison it is, 16 miles to Morrison, can get
there by noon. Fed Fanny in the harness, pulled a handful of alfalfa, a big old woman came on the road to see if we was not
touching her calf.

Denver

The City in Autumn

*The autumn of the year 1890 seemed as prosperous as the spring. But
there were bad omens. In fall of 1890 Wall Street had a small crisis,
which was noted perfunctorily in Denver newspapers. The* Rocky
Mountain News *reported in November that 600 victims of the drought
starving in eastern Arapahoe County were advised not to come to Denver
for lack of jobs there.*[49]

*Emily and Olive found jobs, but not pleasant ones. Emily worked for
Mrs. Samuel Mauck, wife of the manager of the Colorado Plumbing
Company, who abused her, and Olive worked for Mrs. Anfenger, wife of
a prominent insurance man, who scolded her and denied her the use of the
toilet.*[50]

*During her unhappy employment with the Maucks, Emily made ex-
traordinary efforts to get to church on her day off, for both spiritual and
social solace. She attended the First Baptist Church, a large stone edifice
for 1,500 worshipers at Seventeenth and Stout streets. At church she was
treated like a lady by two very important Denver citizens. One was deacon of the church Frank H. Levering of Levering and Mead, attorneys.
The other was Robert S. Roe, owner of the City Transfer Company,
who held positions as Denver fire and police commissioner, state legisla-
tor, and president of the chamber of commerce.*[51]

*In 1891 Denver real estate transactions began a steady decrease. Later
that year and the next, thousands of workers left Denver, unable to find
work in the declining job market. In the summer of 1893 the prosperity of
Colorado and of the country came to a dramatic end with a nationwide financial panic. In Colorado the disaster was exacerbated by the repeal of*

the Sherman Act authorizing government purchase of silver. Mines and smelters closed, banks failed, and real estate millionaires became paupers. In the single year of 1893 Denver lost about a third of its population. By that time Emily had probably gone elsewhere, to begin a new life with a new husband.[52]

September, Monday 15, 1890

Abide in me.—Be ye steadfast

Home again, Ollie so glad to see us, she has done well indeed. That miserable old croon I have to call sister, she is to uterly mean to live in a house, what shall I do with her—she has made Ollie so much trouble telling a lot of lies. The men brought in their washing. I helped her with it, she is just past her period. We was all done, nice. Dannie came from school, had to have 2 new books. He hitched up Fanny, we drove to C H Hardy, got a Hygene. He is Promoted up stairs, acts more like a man. I went to get oats for Fanny, it costs so to get grain. I went to see if I could get Mr Cyphers to build a stable out of old lumber, no, he is engaged 6 weeks ahead. We got home at dusk, had to fix the old tent, the wind has blown it down. Mr Ed Lundburg come.

September, Tuesday 16, 1890

In the world ye shall have trouble

Tried to get breakfast, no wood. I must go again to work, so much & many to keep. Got Fanny ready to go up town, Mrs. Jasper & her daughter Hennie going, we put in a seat, took them to 14 & Cur[tis]. We went to the Fair, got 1 piece bleached Muslin 6¼¢, 55 yards, $3.44, some Black & White Plaid, $4.40, a nice dress for Ollie dear. Went to see Halleck & Howard, got Lath $2.00, Nails 25¢, now we haul them & go to putting on. We drove by Mrs. Corbin, I went in, she got her dinner ready. I waited for Ollie we go to Nickolas to see how old Bally is, he all right, been there 3 months. Now to the Depot to see about the colt Rock, Ric's last colt killed, 1 year old 4 of May, killed the 20 of May, shoulder broke. Hope I can get something. As we come by the lumber yard, got a load of lath, had some nice mellons from Nickolas garden. Made the rines into sweet pickles.

September, Wednesday 17, 1890

Oh taste and see that the Lord is good

Up before light to see what is going on out with Fanny—she loose, gave her some hay, got the step ladder in so Dannie can begin to lath, they both so sleepy, cannot wake them. I got Dannie up, he went to the lathing, finally done by the front door before school time. He seems so much taken up with his school, how glad I try to be. He may change and make a fair man yet.

September, Thursday 18, 1890

Blessed is the man that trusteth in him

I got Ollie up and at the early breakfast, she made griddle cakes, we melted some brown sugar & it made nice syrup. I put some of the Squash I gave Mrs. Nickolas 10¢ for it, we can have a few pies, it will be a change. I commenced to cut out Ollie new Plaid Dress. I do hope she will live long to enjoy her things. Dannie lathed after school—Tis a big job for a small boy, he is at times so good. We put the clothes to soak so can wash. Dannie went for Mrs Shirells few pieces for Ollie, she had taken them to another to do.

September, Friday 19, 1890

My help cometh from the Lord—

I cut more of the cloth for over head, I sewed it together on the machine.

September, Saturday 20, 1890

As poor's yet makeing many rich

We all so tired, did not rise as early as we needed to. I cleaned the lamp, Ollie went to Mrs. Shirell, paid the last 25¢ for Kerosene— Saw Mr Dan Larkins, told him I wanted to see him, he came soon, he would lath overhead if I could get it, I sent Ollie to see if Mrs Jasper would lend me $1.00, yes, she let Ollie have $10.00 to change. Dan came at noon, lathed over head, put up the cloth, I let him have the marble lamb. Ed Lunburg come.

September, Sunday 21, 1890

The love of God is shed abroad in our hearts

Up so late, one of the men from Langdons, the next house, came to get his washing. Ollie had to slip on a dress quick, we could not make the raise of 10¢ in change. We seem more like liveing now that the lath are mostly on. I do pray for work so I can get out of debt, dear Lord hear my petition, only by thy help can I ever succeed. Do send prosperity to me—Ollie had such nice soda biscuits, she can cook so nice, the apple sauce so good, meat, potatoes. Now for morning service, I am afraid we will be late, yes, sermon half done. Childrens Harvest home, baptism of 4 at the conclusion of the service.

September, Monday 22, 1890

Up early, Ollie cant hurry, I must be off. Dannie hurried, got Fanny ready. I have to go to Solomons to sew, I was there at 8, went to work on a flannel suit, dark Green $1.50 to make, awful. Walked home, tired, so tired, put on a few lath.

September, Tuesday 23, 1890

Went again, I cannot earn my salt working for A Z Solomon.

September, Wednesday 24, 1890

Late, I wont get the suit done today, took some work. Dan not home. Ollie came for me to baste, she can do a great deal to lighten my work.

September, Thursday 25, 1890

At work at 8, I must get it done, was till 2, took another, it was grey flannel, 42 inch. I got $1.50. Got a sack of flour. Ollie came to help me today. Dan came to get us, I waited in a grocery by the Curtis st bridge, he came near getting by, he is so deaf. Went at noon to see Liddell, he seemed glad to see me, he will try to get a little for my colt Rock that was killed by the Fort Worth.

September, Friday 26, 1890

At work 7.30, worked hard all day. Ollie came, wore her light cream silk, it looks good to work in. Mrs. Kinnan went home with us. I got 10 lb of Potatoes for 15¢, she let me have 20¢.

September, Saturday 27, 1890

> *The heavens declare the glory of God. And the firmament showeth his*
> *handiwork*

We went 7.30, I helped Dan get the wood by the Fair, sent him
home to get more with Old Fan & Anna, they got some, took
home the suit, must do what I can.

September, Sunday 28, 1890

Up late, made a hasty breakfast, Ollie's bread she made yesterday
light this morning, could not get it ready yesterday, no, the old
nick is in everything sure. Henny Jasper came in twice, she is tag-
ging all of us most of the time, some of us get a tag sometimes.
Dannie broke the whip fooling with her. We went to church, was
late but the childrens harvest home was good, the Motts given
them. Keeping Jesus ever

September, Monday 29, 1890

> *The heavens declare the glory of God and the firmament showeth his*
> *handiwork*

Went at 7, I must go to some place to work, we will starve sure.
Finished at noon, started for some other work, went to Liddell,
got a paper, went to 3 employment places, got a place as nurse in
a Sweed, went back with Ollie, they had a woman. I then went to
the Col employment, got the place at Mrs Dr Burnham's, came
at 5.

September, Tuesday 30, 1890

Oh Dear, so hard, washed all day.

October, Wednesday 1, 1890

> *Shew me thy ways O Lord teach me*

Ironed & a pot roast. I went to the prayer meeting.

October, Thursday 2, 1890

> *Let me grow in Grace O Lord*

Baked Bread, finished Ironing, cleaned the stove, burned myself.
She is not much of a friend to poor folks.

October, Friday 3, 1890

There are differences of belief but the Lord reigns over all
I at it always at 5.30, I have Doughnuts, 2 pies, they nice, she
made a fuss for they stuck to the plate. Soaked my feet 4 nights
this week.

October, Saturday 4, 1890

No use, she is so hard to suit, I cant. Florence came to make a co-
coa nut layer, I must go. Am laying on the bed and trying to think
& write, am so awful tired.

October, Sunday 5, 1890

Up early to work to earn a chance to go to church & our communion once again. I have been away since July. I fixed my satchel to
take with me. After waiting for them to come to their breakfast at
9, I could get the dishes to wash, cleaned the vegetables, get the
roast ready &c, she is so ugly, no use, I am going tomorrow.

October, Monday 6, 1890

Yet a little while and he that shall come will come & will not tarry
Up so early, have to clean some besides the work, it will be the
last, thank the fates. I got Thomases & the man Charleys that
drives Dr Steadmans carriage, 2 washings. Bundled all up, walked
to the Larimer cable from Calafornia, got home at 3. Mrs. Cyphers had been here. I went to get a dress pattern of her, she is a
dear friend to me.

October, Tuesday 7, 1890

He set my feet upon a rock
Cut & tried to fit Hennys dress, she so hard to fit and we have no
patterns, everything scattred since we put on the lath.

October, Wednesday 8, 1890

The words of the Lord are pure Amen
Washed for ourselves, went to our prayer meeting on foot, it raining so nasty. We must go & get Fanny at Nickolas, she out there.
Left so we could get Bally, he so lame, I cried all the way home,
must give him away at last. Oh how hard the fate to me. I must

take a small sum for him so I may get Fanny home again. It is a long nasty walk in the rain, yet I can not stay from my prayer meeting when I can go.

October, Thursday 9, 1890

Pray our father who art in heaven

I went at daylight in the mud to see Dan Larks, he out feeding, Lou in the house, old Tomlinsons, they live as I used to with them, cook & eat at the same table. I had enough of that. She was not put out to live when she was 7 years for nothing, she knows how to "rustle, remember. I got $5.00 for "Bally" a horse. I gave 2 other and $75, in money think of that—for an old wind sucker. Will I ever get free from from the old troubles. Mrs. Tomlinson has 2 children, their mother dead. She thought I might get a child or 2 to keep so I could earn my living. I went out to Nickolas, staid to supper. Dan rode Fanny all the way back. followed car.

October, Friday 10, 1890

Hallowed be thy name, Dear Father

Up late, Olive not well her periods, she has got a cold. We Ironed, cooked some squash for pies, will will have a good dinner for Dan on his birthday. He went after school for a load of wood, got quite a nice lot, we will have to pick up our wood while we have the horse sure. If I could only sell her so as to get her worth, it dont do to try to have others to sell for you. Dan Larkins if she was his would fix it, but he aint so anxious for us. He could trade old Bally the same day he got him. I must go out to work or winter will see us all hungry and naked, I fear.

October, Saturday 11, 1890

Thy kingdom come oh Lord

I got up early, the rest so very hard to get started. I got our Breakfast, soup &c, Ollie's bread light, she has too bake something for her brother birthday dinner tomorrow. He will be 13, such a big boy and tries I think to be good sometimes. We have to finish Henrietta Jaspers dress, it is a job. We must set Dannies quilt together for his present, it is pieced, Annis did it at odd times this summer. Now he will be so pleased to get it. Ollie made a layer

cocoanut cake, cleaned the silver, made apple pie, her bread so
nice. I went to Anna C, took a note of invitation to Edwin
Lundburg to come to Dannies Birthday Dinner, also took home a
part of her beadstead. I cannot buy it.

October, Sunday 12, 1890

Thy will be done on earth as it is in heaven

I let the children stay in bed, they love so to sleep in the morning,
nothing to hinder them from rest. Oh how I do wish I could have
a little help in maintaining my home, I shall dread the cold winter
so much. I dont have verry good success getting employment—
why I get so poor pay for hard work, now I must try for more
work. We have 7 mens washing this week, Henry Jasper's dress
seems to hang on, I hope it will suit her when we get it finished. I
had to let it go to work buttonholes in the daylight, my eyes are
getting so poor. I went with Dannie to morning Church Baptism,
the subject Tupper as a scholarly man, he showed every thing
clear, why if we followed Christ we must be immersed. I came
home, wrote some, commenced dinner. Edwin came, he has a
hard cold—everything went on pleasant.

October, Monday 13, 1890

He that doeth the will of God abideth for ever Be ye holy Amen

Must hurry to go and help Mrs Rodgers. She sent Clara her girl
for me Saturday, I had so much to do to fix for Dannie, I could
not go. I went, she was in the midst of a big washing, I worked
hard all day, hung the washing out 3, and went to sewing, bound
a big comfort. An old gentleman a Mr Burnell boards with them,
how nice he seems, if I could get 1 or 2 such to board I could do
well. I pray god to send me some way so I may stay at home. I
brought some bread as I come, Ollie alone, they Dan and aunt
gone to get Thomas washing, they come, we went to bed early.

October, Tuesday 14, 1890

I up and cleaned the kitchen, such disorder I cannot seem to abide,
why cannot they keep things as I want them. Went late to sew for
Mrs Rodgers, she not a verry particular, she is such a poor house-
keeper but goodhearted. He came at 3 unexpected, she flew out,
got on the wagon, threw out the gun, a rabbit he had killed on his

trip. He said the snow was knee deep in the mountains. She shot off the gun, ripped arround, then here come some of her folks from Lincoln Nebraska, they come to try in Denver for a chance. I am afraid they will not think it is so nice after a few months. Mrs. Rodgers made no change in her supper, she dont care what or who. How I do wish I had a little of what she wastes.

October, Wednesday 15, 1890

Give us this day our daily bread

It snowing hard. I got up, took the broom, swept off the door-step, then went and asked Dan at laws gospel's if I could put Fanny in, he thought I could, so he asked old Langdon, he said yes, he guessed so. We put her in and fed her, Dannie hitched her so I could go down to see about Annis advertising her land. She has lost the paper I had got ready, so I have to see to getting an-other. I got it, went to Liddell, got a check for $5^{00}, he see's I have a hard time to live, went to prayer meeting, hear some of the ter-rible church debt on their hand, we must never try to live beyond our means. Went to 1151 Logan, too late, then 1030 Penn. Ave, I may get it yet, will try tomorrow.

October, Thursday 16, 1890

Forgive us our debts as we forgive our debtors

Got started at our wash, have only a few to wash for besides our own. Dan got all the water and cut a little wood. I left Olive to do the work. I went for a place to work by the week, I must get at work again. We went to several places but I am not going to a place where there is a large family, I must not. I went home at noon, she had the washing out. I had cut Dan a pair of overalls, I made them, fitted Olives black satin waist so she will have a change, she had out grown her old waste, & can fix her skirt, then will have a change. She is doing splendid & can manage as well as I can. If only Dan could see that he can be a man.

October, Friday 17, 1890

Lead us not into temptation, but deliver us from evil Amen

I up at 5, got the rest up, Dan dont like to start. We warmed our breakfast, eat & started to the bakery, got for a nickle 14 coffee rools & a loaf of bread. I found a new suplement, see some chances for Olive & Dan, will all try to see if we can get a start—again too late for the place at Madame Ross for Olive, but she will give us plain sewing, the place 608 16th st[reet]. C Stoll engraving, a boy from Taylor st, our neighbors, got a boy there at 8 oclock, we must be more spry. I tried at several, came out 31st Lafayett comenced at noon for a Mr Sam & Bertha Mauk, they are nice. I have $20.00 per month washing &c. I wish the stove would get off like ours, it dont draw good, what will I do.

October, Saturday 18, 1890

Up at 5, built the fire, got the breakfast—he has been sick but is going to try to go down to his place of buisness to day, he can only eat toast & eggs, seems like a good man, a Plumber & gas fiter. I have bread to bake, will it be good, I pray it will. I cleaned the pantry, the sink & kitchen, washed some for the baby, he is at the neighbors while his 3 yr old brother Maurice is down with the scarlet fever. He fell in a pit filled with ashes, got his right limb fearfully burned. Dr Jenner attends him, she is burning sulphur so that all danger will be avoided. I had a pork roast with sage dressing, cookies, so nice.

October, Sunday 19, 1890

Thine is the kingdom and the power & the glory forever Amen
Got up late. I have to be spry, for she said I could go to church. That is kind. I have everything in nice order, now I got the breakfast all ready, had to wait as usual. They came just as the Dr got here to dress the little boys limb, such a burn from right hip to toe. He is a good boy three years old, so patient, has had the scarlet fever since he was burned. I could not get off till 9.30, got home just 10 from 31st Lafayett. It about 4 mi, the cable is a wonderful thing. Found all nice, they getting ready for church. I changed my dress, we started on time, Annis I gave something to read, she will do all right if she is watched. I came on the cable, found Mrs Mauk cross, she dont like to cook. I prayed so earnest she got over the unpleasant

October, Monday 20, 1890

Up early, Mr Mauck is going to get ready to go east on buisness.

We will have to stay alone, so I shall have the chores & the fires to attend. He said he would give me an extra $1.00 if I took good care of them all. I shall do my best, sure has god at last given me a chance & am I not trying to do his holy will, may I yet have a home. I washed a large washing, 2 quilts, 5 sheets, a lot of baby clothes &c. She is a good woman, treats me so kind. I have a home I do hope for the winter. I got the supper on time, had mashed potatoes, sausage, baked apples. I opened out the sofa, had a better bed. Mr Burt Jones, her cousins husband, here, he is not a good man, his habits of gambling are awful. He is after them to borrow money.

October, Tuesday 21, 1890

The father shall give you another comforter even the holy spirit
Up 5, got their breakfast, he is going this morning. He would have gone last night but had only 20 mi after he was ready. He is so affectionate to his dear wife, why had I no home. Little Maurice lays on his bed and moans after him, that is the way a good kind father & husband is regarded. I made corn meal griddle cakes for them, they were nice. Ironed some, she went to the City, I took care of Maurice, worked on the Bureau cloth for Olive, the Owls I finished, they look so cunning. Maurice is so much care, he dont know how to lie still. His father will be gone 2 weeks or more.

October, Wednesday 22, 1890

I got up early determined to clean the stove in the kitchen, it dont burn good. I took the pipe off, cleaned it out. In the bottom of the back was one of the stove legs, had been their since they came here in May. It was a big ugly job. I got the fire & breakfast by 8, now I will finish the Ironing. Had pork chops for dinner, cleaned the floor. She got flour, apples, grapes, potatoes &c. I take care of everything as if it was my own, she treats me right and I am never one to forget a kindness.

October, Thursday 23, 1890

If anyone have not the spirit they are not Christ
I slep as I do at home, she is glad to have me rest. She treats me

good. I hurried to get the breakfast, griddle cakes, eggs, fruit &c.
I carried the slop out, helped dress Maurices limb. She went down
town to get her dress colored a brown, got her a pair of shoes, a
bonnet frame, for me a black wing, she is going to fix it, I know
she will make it nice. I have the coal &c up stairs. I must quit this
for a number of days. It is near dinner time, I wrote a letter to
dear Olive concerning a place near here, a Mrs. Solomon. We
must both work out, god protect us is my prayer.

October, Friday 24, 1890

He that cometh to me I will in no way cast out.
I up, fire at 5, she still asleep. Finished Olives Owl tidy to day,
made apple pies.

October, Saturday 25, 1890

Live blameless that we may be found without spot, blameless
I have the sponge light for my bread, breakfast does drag, it takes
so long to get through griddle cakes & coffee, eggs for the boys. I
feed Maurice, she feed the baby Raymond. A letter by Telegram,
he is comeing on Wed the 29, they will move to Indiana, her old
home, she is so eager to go.

October, Sunday 26, 1890

We got up late, she said as soon as I got the breakfast over and
Maurice down in the Parlor I could go over & get Fanny so I
could let Mrs Watson take her for the feeding. I hope she will be
as kind to her as she has to the boy Ramon Finker Mauck, she has
had him 4 weeks, has got him as fat as butter. I went, found Olive
gone to church, I got Fanny, Dannie hitched her, in O came, she
had took her things over to 2212 Champa on the 21 Tuesday. Mrs.
Anfenger sent her 2 postal cards, I do hope they will be careful &
kind. She has been home with me 1 year but sees we both have to
work out.

October, Monday 27, 1890

Take heed ye know not what ye are
She got the bath tub, commenced telling me how poor I did the
washing &c. A Telegram from him. Washed a big one, she rinsed
& hung up, they look so nice. She is so nervous, rubbed till she

was all tired out, then went over to Mrs. Watson. I had to leave
the washing, I said I could not be with Maurice & wash to. She
talked verry hard, I never took 4 such blowings up as I have here.

October, Tuesday 28, 1890
Blessed are the poor in spirit
I commenced the day as usual, so long to get through breakfast—
I went to Ironing, I took the baby, found a big black body louse
on him, then we went to hunting, oh heavens we stripped.

October, Wednesday 29, 1890
I trust in thy word, cleanse thou me from secret sins
I finished the Ironing, she run to the Dixons, to the grocer, to
Watson, Maurice screaming so hard. She let me go to see Ollie, I
took Ramon in his carriage, started at 3, saw Mrs. Parker, she had
her baby, Dan she calls him, was making pies, could not care for
me. I left him by the lady where the street car crosses to the
[. . .], carried Anna a loaf of bread. Hurt my feet, a long way.
Was in her house at the ranch 1 year to day, a raging snow storm,
French over in my cabin with Abb & Sam, now they cannot see
us anymore. Fried some apples. Mrs. Bertha Mauck she called me
an adventuress, I could not reason one bit.

October, Thursday 30, 1890
I built the fire, counted 15 big whoppers crawling, I guess this is
the last, my back is so sore. I got dinner, made apple pie, she at
the table. Here he comes, so glad to get to his family. She treats
me all right today. I pray to help me and that now, I am trying. I
sewed for her today.

October, Friday 31, 1890
Do as thou has said. Amen
I swept, dusted & cleaned the whole house up and down, so tired.
Mrs. Watson here all day, they sit and talk, Mrs. Watson has lived
here 20 yr, knows all the old timers, knew father.

November, Saturday 1, 1890
His name shall be called counselor
Such a week, oh Lord, the children to take care of, she down

town with her husband househunt, he dont know what to do, I
am so tired out, I am not able when the days, she let me sleep
down stairs last night, I must rest, she sees that.

November, Sunday 2, 1890

The might god, amen

Cooked a pot roast & dumplins, apple pie, took a basin bath,
changed. Mamie, the girl that worked for them, came, she is a
bold thing, sweed, goes around the house as if she owned it. Mrs
Mauck said after I had dinner I might go home, she gave me the
dry pieces of bread, I am thankful for any and all. I had only a few
minutes to stay. Dan had been home all day, poor boy, his life like
ours is a wreck. Olive was here when I got back, I tell her have a
nickle fare.

November, Monday 3, 1890

The everlasting Father

She so buisy with the uncertainty of what they will do. I cared for
the children both, they done verry well. I am so tired, more so
than if I had done the washing. I went to sleep on her bed as I put
Maurice in bed. They came, I did not hear them. Got the boiler
on, could not do one thing. She went to get her brown dress fitted and made, $5.00 for it.

November, Tuesday 4, 1890

The Prince of Peace

I went up with Maurice breakfast, they playing, she came out of
the little closet crying, she was angry. He paid me $5.00, two
bills, laid it on the bed. 2 $5.00, how I need this & more. I shall
try to please her, so hard, she was talking with him, they are in
some trouble, depend on it. Mamie Oleson, the girl sweed, is
bound to get back if she can. I am washing so big a wash, she is
helping me good.

November, Wednesday 5, 1890

The rich shall be laid low

Mrs. Watson here this morn the first thing, Mrs Mauck down
town with Maurice to get his hair cut. Ironing and tending baby,

how it does hinder me to stop. I try to be patient, Mr Mauck is a cross man, I am always afraid when he is around. I got dinner, dumplins, buiscuit, she brought a pumpkin pie, cracker, cookies. Mrs. Watson again all day, how Mrs M gets one thing done I cant see, potatoes, a basket of grapes. I put M to bed, he wiped the spoon for an excuse.

November, Thursday 6, 1890

Lead me in thy truth O Lord teach me thy way

[Later]: Poor Mrs Keller, her baby boy was born 5 oclock this morning, Dr Hart attending. I did not know them till now, Sat Dec 20.

All seems to go well this morning, I do hope she will be pleased. Watson had an old bed quilt on Fanny, must be she has to stand out. I do wish they could buy. Two men came and got Mamie's trunk, she has given up comeing back. Mr Mauck came at 10, she cross at me for some reason, such talk I never heard to one near twice her age. She seems to loose all sense, then when it is done she says she is sorry and ashamed.

November, Friday 7, 1890

Oh Lord teach me thy way

I up early, got breakfast, called, they not up. I went up, got the baby, brought it down, dress and washed it, then tried to get the breakfast. I moved the table out into the kitchen as she ordered, then she began to find fault, Morrice he began to scream, his father took him, she bounded quick as lightning across the kitchen, hit the child a slap on the head, the father put it down, went over to her, hit her, then she run out of the room, the baby left screaming. Oh such a home, I dont know how I can stand it, I must. He called Mrs. Watson all sorts of bad names because she borrowed some butter. I must be careful, I will. Mrs W came, brought it in 1 hour after the row. I had so much worry with both children. He took her to get a $20.00 cloak.

November, Saturday 8, 1890

Fear thou not for I am with thee and the lord will send his angels

Another day, oh when when will I have my time all to rest, will it ever come, I try to be kind, it does no good. Here comes one of Mrs Watsons girls, Lila, she goes up stairs, down comes Mrs M, what have I said to Mrs W, only that shen she came blundering in yesterday and waked the baby as I was trying to get it stilled, she called she had brought back the butter—that I was glad for her sake, she ought to have more sense. She is going to see if she cant make me a bit of trouble. Mrs M I am sure dont like any better than I do, she & Mr M agree on that. She went over as Mrs W requested, but we will fool her once for a fact. Mrs M says she will give me a good recomend. She says I must take Fanny, all right, I am too glad if only Dannie comes tomorrow.

November, Sunday 9, 1890

I never combed my hair or sat down all day. I lay, for I am not feeling well enough to get up, yet I must. I come unwell last night, I am verry bad of late, my age, must be. I am so glad no more babies for me—I got things in good shape by 8, went up stairs, washed Ramon, dressed him, came down. They came soon, I never know when she will be good, everything went nice so far, now for a big dinner. She is a perfect tyrant on Sunday it seems, wont let a person have breathing room. I cooked chicken, mashed potatoes, made buiscuit, had the both children, think of it, then she came, found fault because I did not put milk in the grava. Dan came, I had stay out door, she was ashamed, went called him in, he had dinner, he took some meat home. *Drove Fanny,* she getting thin. Olive & Edwin came, they such a comfort.

November, Monday 10, 1890

I sought the Lord but found him not

I could scarcely stir my head aches so, no use, must go. She called for coal the 1st thing, I do hope she will not be cross. She seems to be so anxious about her expense, that is right. We washed. The old man that brings the milk, his name Rothwell, his daughter Mrs Waldsmith owns the cow. Mrs Mauck is off with him to Monclair, he has a job plumbing out there, she went for the ride. I took care of the children and washed, had all the clothes, rubbed the flannels out, she helped me get the dinner, then hung out the clothes for me. Mrs Watson came held the baby for us.

November, Tuesday 11, 1890
> *Truly my soul waiteth upon God*
> I am not feeling as well for my hard day yesterday. I got every-
> thing allrite on time, I must do the Ironing. Dinner as usual, she
> went after it with him, gone all the afternoon. I got nearly all
> done, had Ramon all cleaned, they brought liver to cook. I had
> baked potatoes and also apples. He went to get shaved, they have
> tickets for the Play Cinderilla, good. I tended the children till 11,
> got so sleepy, never lay down, patterned off the shoe pocket, let-
> ters, they went right to bed. When I got down to fit my bed I
> found the robe gone, they had it. I took a rug, I got up, it was so
> cold, hunted in the parlor, found it.

November, Wednesday 12, 1890
> *After this manner pray yet Our father which art in heaven*
> I got breakfast under great difficulty, the fire would not burn, I
> put in kindling, the coal is to fine. He is in a hurry, never knew it
> to fail, she is good natured for a wonder, yet if I was not careful
> she would fly of and chew the rag, as he says. Now she is off to
> Mrs Dixons, goes every morning somewhere sure, never con-
> tented at home. I carried the washboard to Mrs Dixon to see if
> Mrs Mauck would come & get the meat, no. I must find some-
> thing. I made some buiscuit, they were nice, she was pleasant,
> nothing to do but I must go up stairs this P.M. I did, she made at
> night a Tappioca apple pudding, I at rest early. Then I got the
> wrong car on 17 ave, had 13 blocks to run, I near dead. Such a
> heavy snow last night, she said I could go home but went away
> then, did not let me.

November, Thursday 13, 1890
> *Our father which art in heaven*
> I had breakfast on time, the children screaming as if they had
> nothing. How I do suffer with it. He says she shall go back to her
> home in Indiana, wont their grandma look to see them so saucy,
> she is off for a 2 hours at Mrs Watson and that after such a talk,
> thank the lord I have the horse back again now, whatever I am
> through. She scolded me again for not putting onions in the meat.
> I could not please her in the morning if she, as he said, got up
> wrong end first. I done all I could, that is sure. He said she would

be sorry as usual. Can I stand so much, that is the question. She
let me go home to get coal for them, I got $2.00 worth of the
Summit Co. Dan is to haul it, Fanny got loose, they say Henny
Jasper caught her.

November, Friday 14, 1890
Hallowed be thy name—
I heard a big pounding on the hall door, he is in a hurry I guess.
Moved all his old fixtures up & in the cellar last night, he is going to stop that office rent now, if they only can find a small house
with a barn so the $20.00 per month horse keep can be changed.
They have a lovely rig, a coal black Prince, young, a nice new
buggy—They are out again today househunting, what a time I
have keeping the 2 boys. Maurice fights Ramon, Oh dear I try to
amuse them. The S[treetcar] C[ompany] is being [beginning]
again now to put the electric car on 31st sure, they have everything ready, have been at work 3 weeks. I think she has found a
house & stable at last, now she can move. I washed all day
Ramons didies, 17, mopped to.

November, Saturday 15, 1890
Thy kingdom come—Amen
Yes, the talk at the table shows they are going to move. She is so
cross I shall go unless she treats me different sure. I cannot stand
such talk as she gets off about my knowing so much. All I try to
do is to please her. I am to go with her to the Cinderella Mattinee
to care for Maurice. I know she will abuse me, this will be the last
time sure. We were just in time for the car, I run to hurry her. I
carried the big boy, was worried and tired as we went up the stairs
in the 15 st Theatre. I dropped off his cap, it is so verry big for
him. Such talk, she abused me as much as she dare. I am going
now, on the way home I see it was to be hotter than ever. I told
Mr Mauck he might pay & I would go, such a scene, she charged
me $1.35 for the bonnet we had made. I must stay awhile, I used
reason.

November, Sunday 16, 1890
Thy will be done

I got sick, she had said finally I could go to church but I am sick. I
took all the Epson salts there was, no use, I am near blind with
the headache. I done the work all day, took care of the boys, they
went out to ride. I lay down on the hall mat upstairs, got to sleep.
I have done up the supper work, am now ready to go to rest. She
is kind now as she can be, I should not mind it if she would be so
all the time. She fried the corn and they eat there supper. I lay
down on the sofa where I sleep. They after supper pulled all the
tacks out of the carpets upstairs & down. My head feels some better.

November, Monday 17, 1890
   On earth as it is in heaven
   I up at 5, he called, they expect a days work. I am no more to
them than an old horse. They are going to move today in a house
2922 Downing Ave. where there is a good barn too, they can keep
their horses now, he pays $20.00 per month for its keep. She is not
so cross this morning but she expects me to git all the same. I got
breakfast over, then washed out the didies, she packing upstairs, I
down stairs, hard at it. The big wagon came at 11, $3.00 for piano
and all. He had 3 loads in his Plumbing wagon, every scrap is to
go, she was sure to give that order. I gathered kindling wood, all
then went over to the place and worked till 11 hard, 3 of the carpets down and a good many things straightened. I had to sleep yet
on the sofa in the parlor, such a hard bed, she seems not to care.
The body lice, such a long seige as I have had.

November, Tuesday 18, 1890
   Give us this day our daily bread
   Yet we must work. I dont feel as if I could do scarce a thing I had
to, life so hard. On the base burner, it is so verry heavy, has to be
cleaned, tis covered with hen drop and rust, has been in the barn
all summer, such a nice stove ruined. I do wish I could have such
nice things, but the Mrs Mauck is jawing away and in a big ugly
fit. Must I go through more of her abuse, yes, she wont try to get
the bedstead set up in the back room, I would get a good nights
rest, that she dont wish.

November, Wednesday 19, 1890

Again I am serving up a nice hot breakfast to a pair of such in-grates. He is the best of the two, that is not saying much. Cleaned the kitchen. She is cross, went to take him to a job, she goes & takes him and brings him home, I have the cross boys to take care of and work. We put down the last carpet and set up the bedstead. I must take that crosspatch of a Maurice in my bed, oh dear wont I be glad when this is over.

November, Thursday 20, 1890

And forgive us our debts as we forgive our debtors

I up and breakfast at 6, he cross, says two old women and nothing done, she put him up a nice lunch. I hurried to get the water over & things ready for a washing. We will have a big one sure. She says I must do it all winter for her, she left the bulk till Monday. Tired to night.

November, Friday 21, 1890

Cleaning the baseburner and the scouring the black kitchen floor, three meals a day she will have. She twits me of getting $20.00 per month but says of late more about my earning it. Yes, I guess I do, I am so tired when night comes. Such a big time to night, Olive came to see me, Mrs Anfinger has gone to abusing her, re-fused her the use of the water closet, such a mean trick. She wanted to see if I was willing for her to leave, yes, she need not take a bit of her abuse—wheeling the old broken baby buggy, get-ting turnips, hurrying them on, making pie and buiscuits &c—she comes in, commences to abuse me, tells Maurice to strike me, he threatens to do.

November, Saturday 22, 1890

And lead us not into temptation

I was going to leave last night but he made her behave. She is like a fiend when she gets started. I shall go tonight as sure as he can pay me which he says he will do. I am so glad to get away. I run to the grocery for her material to make cake, got 3 lamp chim-neys, done the cleaning, got the supper, she never done 1 thing to help me, I done the supper work, then oiled the kitchen floor, then at 10 oclock came to the Larimer cable, came home. He paid

me $5.95 and yet they owe me $2.00, will give it me when I get
home from this ranch trip.

November, Sunday 23, 1890

Sunday morning at home, everything so in a mess. I took down
the stove pipe, it was smoking like a tarkill, cleaned it, then went
over to see if Mr Roger could build me a stable soon if I could get
the boards. I cleaned and fried the fish for her, she made me stay
to breakfast. I washed her dishes, then came home, got ready for
church but it was 12. Stopped at the lumber yard between 9 & 10
that had burned 10 days ago, I can get old board there, no, they
are all gone. Now I must go and try Halleck & Howard, if I can
get enough to make a place 8–10, it will have to do. Dannie took
a little walk, had a chance to earn a nickle, he then took me over
to Mrs Maucks to wash for them on next day.

November, Monday 24, 1890

But deliver us from evil for thine

Up early. Maurice was restless, wanted me to give a drink milk 4
times. She worried with Ramon, I got the breakfast, he in a hurry
to go to his work Plumbing. She is going to take him, I will see
to the boy's for her. I got at the washing for her before she got
home, a big one—done by 1, but she wanted me to stay till
morning, so I said I would. I kept the boys while she went got her
dress & saw an old Mrs Hall that want to come to work for her
board. She will do, I think, for a while. I cleaned the floor, then I
changed my dress, got on the turnips, the apples &c, she brought
the bread, we had a pleasant meal, she wrote me a verry nice rec-
ommend.

November, Tuesday 25, 1890

Is the time to come I can be again free to go where I will? I went
to Liddells to see what I had to do to save the little I have. He
gave me the deed & told me to go the Co Clerks office, have it
entered as a homestead in red ink on the margin of the record. I
walked from Tabors block to the court house and back, then over
to 2230 when Olive is at work Anfingers. She is going to stay, so
she says. Edwin think it best, she is going to pay $5.00 on the
lumber act—then I went to see at Mays & Appells for a hat &

boots for Dan, then about lumber for the stable, then home all afoot. I eat a little, then up to the school for Dan. It is over in a small frame, the teacher name Miss Hutchison, he must be out now to go with us to the ranch.

November, Wednesday 26, 1890

Is the kingdom and the Power

I over to help Lou Larkins, she sick again, flowing. I washed her dishes, took the ashes up, then made me a cup of tea, eat a few bites, then spilled the tea, went to the bakery, got cakes & cheese for the trip, 15[¢], then home, got all ready to start, now the worry begins. He put on the washers (25[¢]) the harness must be mended 30¢, I got the bill for the lumber for the stable, $8.86, paid 4.00 on it, got Dan's boots & hat, all $2.50. The plasterer came just as we started, said they would put on 2 coats on the bathroom for $12.00. I then had to go to see if Lou Larkins would see to it that my goods were put away. I will get her a calico dress. We bid Mrs Corbin good bye 3 oclock, I gave Mrs. Long-fellow 50¢ more than I had to.

November, Thursday 27, 1890

We at a Mrs Ead's on the ditch, old John Nickolas had the good-ness to say we could have started in the morning & we could go to a house back, *never*. We got a good place, slept on the floor but that is all right—Thanksgiving, yes, we ought to be glad tis as well with us as it is, we have health. True, sister has neuralgia in her face, Dannies eyes are weak from Measels, but we will do the verry best we can. Now at 9[00] we are on the road, will go as far as we can, eat lunch after we passed the town Sullivan, all built since I was on the road, stoped & fed Fanny at the white house by the bridge, Cherry Creek, Ned Melvin. Got a cup of tea and a good lift for the ranche, we wont starve sure.

["Letter Register"]: Elizabeth, Thursday, Nov 27, 1890, at Mrs Wests. I wrote a hasty letter to Olive, Louie Larkins and Henny Jasper to see to it if the things had to be taken out of the home while I was up here at Elbert.

November, Friday 28, 1890

And the Glory Forever & ever, Amen

Stoped after dark at a little cabin 4 miles the other side of Elizabeth, Mr Schepps, nice German folk. Dan said he could see a light, we said no but go see. We laid on the all the floor, we saw not over 5 feet, Anna sat by a box and slept. They made corncake & mush, I had tea—now on the road, we have a sack of corn for the horse, we stoped at Mrs West's, she made us come in, have dinner. I wrote to Olive, to Lou, to Henny Jasper, then took hold & washed. She has more than she can do. We started 1.30, Dan went over to see Agnes Clibon, she lives in Elizabeth. Now for the ranch, got there at dark. We have been favored all the way. I sneezed, tis danger.

November, Saturday 29, 1890

Everything as we left it, but they have made a road on her land. He drove in as if he was lord of it all—never mind, we will see now. We have to see to it that the out house and chicken house are put up, the barn is all right, we put Fanny in last night. We have done some work, will get dinner. We have a pot of beans & meat, a good lot of bread & some flour. We went at evening to Mrs Fricks, she so glad to see us. We had some milk, she put a matrass on the floor and we had a lot of quilts & blankets. I dreamed I had 7 letters, counted them over, saw strangers, *sneezed.*

November, Sunday 30, 1890

By their fruits ye shall know them, not every
I got up early, made the fires for Mrs. Frick, she asleep. I got both built, then made the bed off the floor. She got a nice breakfast, coffee, potatoes, meat & grava, bread, butter, good. Wallie Whiting came, told Dan he would give him a pup bull dog breed. We started, she gave me the keys to a padlock on her gate, we could not turn the key. We got water at Mrs. Killian, she such an old fudge bug. We drove on to Mr Sloans, they glad to see us, got dinner, tea, meat, potatoe, buiscuit, we to bed 8.30. We spent more than 1 hour getting over the fence, had to lay 2 posts down.

December, Monday 1, 1890

Up at 8, Mr Sloan built the fire, a good potatoe stew for our breakfast. She has not much, they good but poor. Dan got the horse, we have to get my rubber shoes at Mrs Holdens at Bijou

Basin. Mr Sloan drove old Fanny as far as Mr Knights, Dan rode
Dic, the white horse, then he got in and drove for me. We stoped
at Mrs Mary Shillinger Mather, they all well. Found Mrs Holden
gone to her daughters Mrs Durkee, I got the rubbers, newer than
the ones I left there. I started on, stoped at Mrs Phillipps, her
daughter Edith got us a can of rich milk, then on the way back we
got a few sticks of wood for Sloans, tis not much we can do but
some. He gives Fanny corn stalks. We got back to dinner all right,
I not feeling well. I had a nice corn meal mush. After supper mended Dans pants, always tore.

December, Tuesday 2, 1890
One that sayeth lord lord shall enter into rest
We carried the bedsted last night, Mr Sloan yesterday fixed her
kitchen & closet tool room, I took unwell in the night. Sister had
3 hard Spasms, Anna so sick, Fanny Dan rode near to death to get
D McNelan, he said it was nervousness. She fell down stairs and
hurt her spine 20 years ago, went in the cold to Mrs. Finch for
milk to give sister. I so bad I can scarcely go, blood like water. He
was so verry good as to bring her an old chair. To the Mathew
ranch to water Fan and get 7 cans for our use, and plenty of water
at the next house to her. I unwell so bad 1 week too soon. In
Hammonton she got the fall.

December, Wednesday 3, 1890
Lord shall enter into rest
We at work hard to get fired, the wind awful, seems as if it would
blow the house down. We could not scarce keep warm. I am bad
with my monthly sickness—yet I must do for the rest, Dan does
all he can, poor dear boy, where will this all end.

December, Thursday 4, 1890
But he that doeth the will of the master
Breakfast, cornbread, tea, milk, we all slept together on the floor.
Annis better, no poison. I am bad unwell but must do all I can to
get things up. Sorted old letters, Dannie saw so many of his fathers dear expressions it will last him all the rest of his life, such
lying & dissembling, has been all his mean life since I ever knew

him. I baked buiscuit, cake, tapioca, stewed raisins in, also cooked
dried peach, we have butter & milk potatoes. We had a good lot
of food, lay down to sleep having thanked God it was as well
with us as it was.

December, Friday 5, 1890

Up early, breakfast, tea, cake, potatoes, *salmon* that we brought all
the way from Dake. We did not think when we packed up to go
from there we should eat them at Annis ranch. We are nice but it
is so cold up here. I will be glad when this is all over and I can go
back to Denver and get to work. Drove over to see if Wm. Green
would not come to see Annis at the ranch, since the buildings
were moved, yes, he would and sure he came while I was gone,
told her that she was all right, had $500.00 improvements. Drove
old Fanny to Kiowa, 9 oclock when [. . .] My brand ELF not recorded.

December, Saturday 6, 1890

The meekness and gentleness of Christ

Such an uncomfortable bed, bread & milk for breakfast thanks to
Laurie Oaks, she is working so hard. I got things picked up so we
can go home now, put them into the buggy, this is the last of any
of my good's at the ranch. I loaded Annis into the buggy to take
her down to Mrs Griffins, she is a good friend to us, has done all
she could for sister when she was all alone. Her soapstone she has
hot & nice under her feet, so she cannot get cold. We will take her
where she will be comfortable till we can go to Denver, that will
be soon I do hope—we all eat dinner at Sam S. Griffins, he came
in from the store with Joe Purden, both looked ugly. She had my
eardrops in, she hurried the dinner. I went to see Dr McNelan,
then Mrs Baltzell, not at home, to Mrs Cowdrys, wrote to
Mrs. Mauck. Dannie & I went home, left Annis, we told Rev Self
we would be back to morning service sure.

December, Sunday 7, 1890

He will feed his flock

Such a cold raw morning, we can never get down to Church in
time for service, so bitter cold. We put the sled, blackboard, com-

mode, 2 small boxes, sack potatoes, baskets &c. I will never drive
to Elbert, no, we turned Fannys head toward Elizabeth, will put
the things with Nan West. We was nearly frozen, at 1 fed Fanny,
good old brute, Mrs. West got dinner for us, started on 2 30. Have
to go to the ranche now, forgot the axe & the affidavit I got Lee
Ramsey to make last Friday concerning killing of Rock by the
Fort Worth train. Got to Foote pasture at sundown, found the lost
strap, then to the ranch, Annis ranch, 6 years of hard life she has
been there, the old heathen he wants everything. We have good
bye, we are not sorry to go, every thing speaks plain of long and
fearful suffering. To Elbert, we got her in the buggy, started over
to Fricks when tipped over by crick.

December, Monday 8, 1890
I will be as the dew to Israel
Anna so bad sick, 11 at night. Up, combed, washed all of us before her breakfast, it good, Annis eat good. Then I wrote to
Olive, I got a letter from her, she could not unlock the house,
now how will I find things not done. I sewed some, wrote a letter
to the Golden Eagle for Mrs Frick, then we had dinner, Annis
bound to go to the table. We took her out, she eat ravenous, then
droped off to sleep on the table. We, Dan & I, got her to the
lounge, then sudden again she had 2 more of the strangest spasm's
I ever saw. I sent quick for the Dr, he gone, Mrs Frick help, she
came out of them. We got ready, soon 3 ocl, must go as far as
Deitricks to night so it wont take so hard a pull tomorrow. Oh dear,
it seems this trip is so hard, why must it be? We got here, they
welcomed us as nice. Cats, only 10, some on the table. I am at
this book, 11. Fed alfalfa, I am so afraid Fanny is not used to the
stuff. Dan went out to slide with the boy, 2 girls.

December, Tuesday 9, 1890
Dust thou art and unto dust
Up at 5.30, Bertha & Minnie Dedrick hurrying to get ready for
school, they go to Kiowa. We must hurry too, we started as soon
as they. When we got as far as the bridge they come to meet us
and hurry us up. They all there & ready, we went in, the room
full. Ab, Sam, Chauncey & Old F., the whole tribe there. They

must have come Monday night to old Mother Myers, the dirtiest hag in the country. Abbie has lost all shame, poor girl. I got the men to take Annis out into the hotel. Mam Hurtle had the meaness to put her in the office—I put on a can of water, I made some tea and gave them dinner. Chauncy had to sneak in while I was in the land off and tell Dan to come and see him at Bar City: she the men carried to the office in the chair. I had to get our fees, $5.10 each, then we started for Elizabeth, she weak but all right as yet. Got to Mrs Wests after dark, she would get supper, hot coffee, cake. She made a bed on the floor. I fear Chancey has set Dannie on fire.

December, Wednesday 10, 1890

Thou shalt return Behold I have

Up at 5, she said twas to early but twill be 10 before we start, I am sure. Such a good breakfast, she is so kind. We had pork, my potatoes, tea, new bread. She gave a loaf with raisins in it, was burned some, Mrs. Boston gave me a feed of hay, I put in a sack, had the black board, a flour barrel cover, her commode, 2 full boxes, sack potatoes, some feed, the stool & satchel, a full load, 4 quilts, 2 baskets of victuals, all given by my friends. We set very close and uncomfortable. Fanny goes good. From Elizabeth we got to the Howard ranch, they had an empty bed, we stayed all night. To full for a lot to come ride. I thought I would walk up the hills to make it light for Fanny, the 2nd at whiskey gulch. I had put my under teeth in my pocket, I got on, they broke then.

December, Thursday 11, 1890

Thou shalt return, Behold I have created a new heaven & a new earth

I got up 5 oclock, made the fire in the middle room, then in the kitchen. He brought up the potatoes, up and off for home. I got a can full of milk new off 4 cows, I got a piece butter, some cold buiscuits. Dannie must have lost his overcoat yesterday, we cant find it this morning anywhere, what next. We left at Shepp a lot of pictures for their wall. I made buiscuit for them, they so good, the men, 1 Howard, eat hearty. I done up the work, swept all the rooms good. The potatoes out all night & they not frozen. Annis eat in her bedroom, wet the floor bad. We got home 3, Mrs. Corbin so glad, gave us the key's, not one thing done she tell me. I knew it would be so.

December, Friday 12, 1890

Thou renderest to every one according to their works

At 4 I up, I cannot sleep, so much to do. Got our poor breakfast, I helped her get 2 pails water, fried her meat & fish &c, stayed to supper there. Dan asked me to eat, I went to ask Vic Longfellow if he could help. I went over at daylight to see that Dan Larkins has the lumber hauled for Fannys stable. He got the boy Jesse Tomlinson to go for it, he charged $1.00, mean. Jesse Tomlinson took his express wagon, got all the bill called for, the load so heavy I walked. Hauled 600 Canyon City coal, 1.00 for us. Not one bit of kindness in any of them, Lou the one now to try to have them be fair. I must have the window changed to the west, so dark. Epleys Flats near.

December, Saturday 13, 1890

Rogers or Wright shot at a man, never come. I up not so early, only scraps to make our breakfast, oh God will this never get any better. Went over to Mrs. Corbin, she got her head tied up, another of her hard sickheadaches, poor woman. She gave me 3 loaves of bread, apples, meat, tea, *cheese* a big piece, sour milk &c, so good. I got ready quick to go down town, Mr. Wright came to do the little carpenter work, change the window &c, said he would be back by 11. I went to St Marys academy to see Florence Frick, took her a new pair of stockings, she so pleased, dear girl. Dannie waiting out in the buggy, I let him get out, go for a nickle of scraps meat. I went to see Mrs. Mauck, she dont want me to wash next week, but to work soon a week or more. She paid me $1.25, had no more. I went next to Terrys, got hay and ground feed, then to Kistlers, he gave me a pair of shoes. The land office refuse Annis proof, letter not read right.

December, Sunday 14, 1890

Marvle not that I said unto you ye must be born again

Up at 6, must go speak to the little old Englishman that is to fix Annis's beadstead. I want him to fix the sockets for the castors sure. Dan built the fire, we had meat, potatoes, bread, tea, are so thankful. Larkins & Jesse Tomlinson, Ellis Van Osdell, Lou's brother come to lath the kitchen. I have to allow them to do it today for cant get it done in time for the plasterers. They are at Mr Epleys Brick, 5 houses east of me, they will plaster for me when tis ready. They went at noon, only done overhead, I swept up. Olive came, she brought the $5^{00} receipt for the money she paid H. & H., God bless her. She played on the organ, I cut Dans hair, she got the silk patch Aunt Annis made her to give to Mrs Anfenger. We, O Annis & I, got ready & went to church. Frank the janitor carried her up, Mr Coolidge helped me. A good sermon to young men on the 5 great evils that got hold on them & ruin their lives and not them alone, their mothers.

December, Monday 15, 1890

I sat and wrote in this till I was so cold & sleepy last night. Dan snoring, I up as early as ever this morning, made up the last flour and small loaf. We was eating, in come an Insurance man, he talked as they all do, no use, I say no to everything. Then Mr King came to change the window into the west, the old huzzy Longdon out making wry faces, but I have a right to do as I will with this my home. I cleaned the window, went down to the Bakers, got 2 loaves coffee cake, left them to Sniverlys, went to the land office to see to this new trouble, her notice must be published again. To Liddells, he will loan me the $5.00, to Drury, teeth not fixed yet, to Shirrells, got a good barrel, then home. Dan at work, he could not get the place for me. I got 2 men at the stable, could not find my saw.

December, Tuesday 16, 1890

Thou art no more a servant but an heir of God through Christ

Verry cold, did not rise till daylight, Dannie built the fire, I got up, went to see if Fanny was all right, poor old horse. I cant get the stable built, all I can do. I got Mr Longfellow to come & show us how to fix the sides and he put in a 2 x 4 by the middle door, we can go on lathing now I guess. I tried again to get the stable built, no use. I must build it or twill not be done. Mr Jonathan Longfellow is the only one that even will look. This Daggett, the

Carpenter in the Epley's Flats will, if he gets done tomorrow, help a little. The little Englishman Sylvester brought the beadstead cut down, now so I can put it up. Dan hurried on lath, twill hardly get done this week, I fear. Old Sylvester came & told me a man was stealing my boards [Later]: *twas him*. I went to see Mr & Mrs. King.

December, Wednesday 17, 1890

I got up at 3, thought it was morning, got out in the cold, looked for crawlers, found 2 small ones, Annis 5 yesterday. Made coffee, cooked oatmeal, we eat them at the lathing. Old Dan Larkins rode the white horse he got from me round, but he wont do nothing to pay for it. I went to Mrs Corbins, she said come get a loaf of bread. A Mr Cross came to see if I wanted a well and pump put in, I cant do anything, no *money*. Dannie at 11 oclock went to sawing the frame of the new stable 10 x 12–10 feet high. All the help I could get was Charley Johnson & 2 other boys. A woman at the house across the alley she let me have 3 scantling, I had 9 but not enough to make a good strong frame. One of her hens got in the lumber and killed, I got it, Annis cleaned it, put on to cook, we so hard up.

December, Thursday 18, 1890

They that come unto me I will in no wise cast out Amen
Waited till daylight, it is verry cold, we cannot do much, no use so I let Dannie lie & rest—we had a little milk, I warmed the coffee, no meat but that old hen. Annis pealed some potatoes, put in, good. Mrs Corbin let me have a piece of an onion, 2 fried sausage, some bread, 3 cakes &c, what could I do without the little she gives us. I have to hunt Fanny, I went down to the Bakery, he gave me a sack of old bread & cake, such a help sure. When I came back Old Fan was gone. I went over the whole Chene Dago outfit, then as I was about to go to the pound, there she stood in Everett's barn filling her old self. I went down, got 5 bunch lath, sugar, of the land office, my teeth of Drury. A German worked 2 hours lath. Saw Judge Liddell, got $5⁰⁰, he says I need not pay till I am out of debt, how kind.

December, Friday 19, 1890

Had such a good nights rest after the German came & helped lath
so much. Dan can sure get it all done in time. I went to see Mr
King if he wont cut that small door in the kitchen for to let sister
in & out. I had another long hunt for Fanny, she will starve unless
I go out to work. Dannie is working good. I went to the office,
no mail, to Mr Epleys to offer to clean the Terrace, he so pleased.
His sister so nice, she said she should come to see us. I then went
to get Dannies school books, this is the last day of the old year.
His teacher, a Miss Cordingly, had his books put in a desk safe. I
left them, they had a flag raising at the brick school on the Boulevard, I hurried, she gave a Christmas card for Dannie. I went at
dark to let Fanny eat some, Fanny eat hay, saw a good horse
down, came home, went to Mrs Kellers to see if they wanted me,
yes, I will go.

December, Saturday 20, 1890

*Fear not little flock for it is the fathers good pleasure to give you
the kingdom*
Cleaned her floor this afternoon. I got up as the bell tolled 6 ocl,
Dan did not want to but did it. So verry cold, we must put the
siding in the window or we shall freeze sure. I got our small
breakfast, tea, oatmeal, soup &c. Must go to Mrs Corbins, she is
keeping me from starvation now, God bless her. She is haveing
the house cealed, she gave me milk, bread, a few Wenewists for
Dannie, said he might come next Wednesday & Saturday & I put
some of my things upstairs. Had Dan to nail the studding in the
stable. I went down with old Fanny to get hay & got a 60¢ bale
and 3 fork fulls of Terry. Drew at the German Nat. $5.00 by
Judge Liddell, the last he may let me have maybe. Got a bunch of
lath at H. H., also some strips, home, I eat a hasty dinner. Now I
take my satchel, Dan not home, go to Mr Kellers to work,
cleaned her floor this afternoon. The Englishman came for his
50¢, I could not let him have it, he will have to take the horse.

December, Sunday 21, 1890

Sat up and mended till 11 last night. The men Mr Keller and Adelbert over to the brickyards where they used to work & they cant

get paid. I got their breakfast, beaf & broth, bread & tea. I slept
with her, she is a skeleton in flesh, has been sick in all 8 weeks, the
boy baby was born Nov 6, I cleaned the house, no cupboard,
nothing, verry little food, but I have to do the best I can these
days. Oh what a hard buisy year this has been for us all. I will not
clean all day this new years day, I did it last in the old Frick house,
Sloan set a light of glass for us, saw Olive & I at work, said we
would work hard all the year, it has been so true. I cleaned Grandma Phelps hair, it white & a thick scab on the scalp. I pealed potatoes, cooked with the beef, had diner 4 ocl, then started home to
go to eve Church. Dann got near done with the lathing, we got
there early.

December, Monday 22, 1890

We should not trust in ourselves, but in God which raiseth the dead
Amen
Up at 5, must hurry & go over to my place in time to go to washing, a big days work, everything in the house dirty. I shall carry a
sheet, some pillowcases for Annis, the tea towels &c so *verry
dirty*—Mrs. Keller said I could do them, then I got all of the
clothes done by 5, put the white in water, carried 10 pails across
the road from a brick house where Mr. Scott, the man that has
been running with Mr Strong, the brick yard's near, they cannot
get any money for 1 days work and they worked 3 months. To
bad. I will wait for my pay, they are so poor. I eat a little supper.
Grandma has done the work all day, poor old woman, she has
never had a chance to be good to herself, I know. I try to favor
her all I can. I carried a big roll of paper near 75 lbs in a sack, twill
cover the barn roof.

December, Tuesday 23, 1890

Got up with a headache so bad, must get things in shape to go
soon to work. We carried the Bureau into the little kitchen and set
Ollie's trunk on it until the plaster is dr[y]. Everything is torn up
and moved out and will be for 3 weeks I fear. I went to my work,
6 oclock, carried some sour milk, got a can of soda for them 10¢,
I carried it and came near freezing my fingers, it verry cold now—
got the white clothes out on the line and the line full, all the flan-

nels dry over night. I killed more than 100 big crawlers sure, they
so *thick,* can I get rid of them? I shall try. I mended and then
washed Annie's red dress, some of the good garments Mrs. Close
got for them. Her tent was burned to the ground Friday night,
Stanley her boy dont seem to care. I got my hair combed & off
5.30, better than I feared. They, Mr Keller & Annie come soon, all
ready to go to the church, had a good time.

December, Wednesday 24, 1890

He is our peace, our Salvation

I got up as the 6.30 whistles blew, am home for they have no
place for me to sleep. The *crawlers are bad,* got a pillow & blanket
to carry & go put things away for Daniel. We got home last night
at 10 from the tree, the church full, Dan in his class for the first in
4 months, poor boy, we live so far away—work all the week so
hard, no use, he never goes in time when the S.S. was in the
P.M., twas the same, never on time—the Magic Lantern Views
were a failure last night in part, not clear more than ½ of them.
Calvary or Jerusalem verry dim. The song "Beulah Land" *nice,* so
several others. Mr. John Keller came with Annie, I asked them.
Fanny pulled us all to the church, Annis went, 5 in all. She goes
every time I can take her, she does begin to see I do all I can for
her. The tree down stairs was nice, every child got a box of cream
candy, a dish of Ice Cream & cake. I went in to help Old Mrs.
Riley, the old thing there always on hand.

December, Thursday 25, 1890

Thanks be unto God for his unspeakable gift

2 ocl I up to get the bottle of milk for the baby, the fire low, I sat
down to put the pages in this from the 21st—this is the first night
I have had a bed to myself, he brought the cot, I brought my bed-
ding. The room is to warm but that I will try to stand it. This is a
hard place at the best, but I must try to bear it. They, Mr Keller &
son, moved the organ, lounge & writing desk into Mr Epleys
house. Dannie came home with them, he stayed to dinner. We had
a baked rice pudding, boiled beef, tea, milk, thanks to Mrs Wier
that lives on the hill we can have all the skim milk at the house we
want. A neighbor brought another gift of mush, beef and some

new shirts for the children, red & white knitted, so warm for them. Dannie played for 3 hours with Chester & Annie and their new Christmas toys, a set of dishes and a train of cars, candy, a wagon &c. Dan is happy as can be, poor boy—The wind at 9 oclock is rageing wild but I know they are all right at home. I went carried meat, potato parings to Fan.

December, Friday 26, 1890

He is able to save to the uttermost all that come unto God by him amen
Up at 5, got breakfast, cooked potatoes, made buiscuits. He, Adelbert, got to go to work at the brickyard shoveling. Grandma cross, she 76—she saw my buiscuits, they so nice, all done at 7, then I brought 10 pails water to wash another batch of clothes for her, poor woman, I comed her hair, she sat up the first time in 8 weeks. She is a skeleton quite, I hurried up her hair, made the beds, then took the top layer of dirt off, cleaned both rooms, got skim milk from Wiers, minute pudding not much else. Mr Keller has head & back ache, lay on the bed till noon, went in the P.M. to the trial the busted brick yard, the Summit. Got the team, I got 2 2 x 4 all the way, so heavy. Dannie left home at about 9 this morning, 3 days gone, he has gone to Barr City I know.

December, Saturday 27, 1890

Mr Rogers after me, wants me to nurse & do the work. I went up to Kellers, got my dress & blanket, they so sorry. How I have to hurry arround, the baby Earl Raymond has a fearful face, scabbed all over thick. I shall do as I wish others to do by me. Again the men put the organ & writing desk into Epleys Flats and lounge, everything all tore out. Oh *dear dear* we are left by Dan, why now, for more trouble sure. I have to go get Olive's trunk and a bail of hay, poor Fanny, she is half fed. I have put up the poor old barn, tis better than none. Mrs Rogers let me go, a Mrs. Dunlap & husband & brother Cash live in the front, no use. Mr Davidson, cousin of Rogers, helped some, I got down on my hands & knees, cleaned the kitchen good.

December, Sunday 28, 1890

Now we see through a glass darkly then face to face amen

Up, had his breakfast 6, he has to switch all day, not any rest on the R.R. I got milk for ourselves, too. Such a place, that old croon, is it any wonder Dan run away, no *no*. A layer queen cake and a pot roast for dinner, I must do all I can to let my neighbors see I care sure. I all so nervous I can scarcely go, carried an orange, 3 apples home, Annis in bed 10. Here is Ike Grewell, says he will take Fanny. He run her after hogs all over town then brought her back for me to feed *oh oh*. The paper concerning Annis land came from Patterson, the affidavit, now will she get it, *yes,* she signed. I taken unwell *so bad,* too often these days.

December, Monday 29, 1890

3, up and scrawling this. Must wash & bake today sure. Mrs Rogers tries to be kind, she is a strange woman, loves god, sings hymns to her baby boy Earl Raymond, yet she is a gossip, speaks ill of most. Because she is a neighbor I try to help. Mr Keller moved the organ & lounge into Mrs Spencers for me. I brought artesian water to do the flannels, also enough to wash the white clothes. Went over to see Fanny. Mr Epley had given two big doors to close the barn, good of him. Mr Roberts come, asked me would I please set on his dinner, *certainly.* I did, then washed while they eat, got done, all on the line, the line untied, down went everything in the sand, such a mess. Cash, Mr Dunlap's brother, helped me up. He cant go with Ollie. I went to the City hall for Dan.

December, Tuesday 30, 1890

Draw nigh to God and He will draw nigh to you
Came last night at 10 on the Larimer cable to Mrs. Mauck's. I rung the bell no 1 heard me. I went to the side window, ra[p]ped, Mrs. Hall she came finally in her night-dress, opened the door, she looked so ugly, does not see any good in any one but her self. I got the water on to wash, went out to wait on Maurice. The man she is going to work for came for her, she has a pile of dirty clothes. Mrs Mauck told her she had to do them herself, good. She took the floor, I never rubbed a bit till half past 10, could not get them on the line till 3. Mrs Mauck so sick all the time I fear she will not live through this so fearful operation. He seems so

ugly but I think he is sorry he acted so mean Saturday last. She had Dr Clark perform an operation to rid her of a 2 month feotus.

December, Wednesday 31, 1890

I up at 5.30, the fire kindled, breakfast ready. We put up Mr Maucks lunch, he went in 1 hour, he came back, some other buisness is at hand. I done the work up, then ironed. She not so pleasant as I supposed she would be but it is all right, I made up my mind to go to the house, I will get supper. She sent me to the grocer for tea. I cooked cabbage, potatoes, she pasted pictures in the scrap book Maurice got for Christmas. The wind on a perfect tare, every thing is blowing away, stove zinc rooling, pipe flying. I started to prayer meeting, must get Fanny some hay, Annis some water, 3 pails, a Mr Gibbs will help, he at Mrs McKillups across the alley, soap *carried home. Old year goodbye.* Oh here is Dannie

		MEMORANDA		
Jan.	1st	Josie Oaks brought hay & oats	$2.00	Jan. 4
	2	Mrs Baltzell came to pay	7.00	I paid
	"	Annis paid me	7.00	$2.00 for
	8	Mrs Baltzell paid	1.00	Olive's
				fare to
				Denver

		CASH ACCOUNT	Rec'd	Paid
Jan.	1	from my witness fee	$5.00	
	2	whitewashed Mrs Fricks corn meal		.45
	3	washed for Mrs Oaks on act	1.00	
	9	" " " " "	1.00	
	16	" " " " "	1.00	
	23	" " " " "	1.00	
	29	took a vest Balty Gaylor	.50	
	30	washed	1.00	
Feb.	5	washed & Ironed	1.25	

	28	the washing after she died	1.50	[1 marked over 2]
Mar.	2	washed 10 sheets &c mended	1.50	
	19	"	1.00	
	21	mended all day	.75	
	24	" " "	.50	
	26	washed all day	1.00	

			[rec'd]	[paid]
Jan.	8	washed Baltzells	1.00	
	14	put a rug on the frames for Mrs Frick on rent	5.00	
	16	got 25c oatmeal 10c envelopes 10c postage		.45
	21	put a rug on for us not paid		
	22	washed at Baltzells buggy	1.00	
	24	cleaned ~~Baltzell~~ meat	~~.25~~	
	25	ironed	.25	
	29	washed all day cleaned	1.00	
Feb.	20	Washed (took my buggy to be painted)	1.00	12.00
	21	Ironed 25		
Mar.	5	doll carriage		3.00
	11	washed all day	1.00	
	13 & 14	1 day ½ ironed	1.25	
	15	ironed got a load of goods from ranch	1.00	
	25	washed & ironed	1.00	

CASH ACCOUNT—July

	15	of Mr J. Jamison of Buffalo Park	5.00	
		of Mrs. Chapman, Webster	5.00	
	16	paid Longfellow		5.00
		Halleck & Howard		4.00
		1 sack flour 25 lbs		1.00
		potatoes & sugar		.50

CASH ACCOUNT—August

25	Michael OBrien	10.00
27		1.15
	Kinear	.50
	Myers	.50
	Mrs. Kelley	.75
	Godfrey	1.25
	Eva Conklin	.25
	Mrs. Dake	2.00
20	of Mrs. OBrien	1.15
29	for wash Mrs OB	1.12

CASH ACCOUNT—September

1	Mrs. Dake	1.50
5	" "	1.25
	sent Olive E.F.	5.00

CASH ACCOUNT—November

4	Mr Mauck the first I have had in 3 mos	10.00
9	he gave me for horse feed	1.50

SUMMARY

	Cash on hand Jan. 1 had $200	5.00
	8	1.00

Epilogue

In the 1891 *Denver City Directory,* Emily L. French was listed as a nurse living in Fairview on the south side of Monroe Street near Main. She may have been living with her reliable friend Mrs. Corbin, for that address was given in the *Directory* as the site of the Corbin Dairy. She had probably lost her house on Willow Street, a block north of the Corbin Dairy, to creditors.

Emily appears no more in Denver directories, and she may have left Colorado as early as 1892. When Marsena applied on February 15, 1892, for a final certificate to the homestead near Elbert where he and Emily had lived together, Emily contested his entry, claiming her homestead rights as a wife. As a result Marsena's application was canceled on July 16, 1894, and he relinquished his right to the homestead. Emily failed to follow up her claim, because sometime between 1892 and 1894 she had gotten married.

On August 13, 1894, Marsena applied again for the same homestead, his claim still stated to be subject to the preferential right of Emily L. French, or as she was now known, Emily L. Varney. Marsena made an affidavit that "Emily L. Varney is a married woman, living with her husband, is not the head of a family, and is not qualified to make entry for said land." In marrying again, Emily had lost her right to the homestead. Marsena was granted a final certificate on October 25, 1894.[53]

Emily's marriage to Mr. Varney is not recorded in Denver. In

fact Emily does not appear in marriage, divorce, assessment, probate, or judicial records of Arapahoe County after 1890. The 1900
census records (which are indexed by last names) do not locate
Emily French or Emily Varney in Colorado, Iowa, or Michigan.
The 1910 census is not indexed, but it shows at least that Emily
was not living in Denver in 1910; the 1920 census enumerations
are still not open to research. Emily does not appear in Colorado
directories for Denver, Elbert, Leadville, Cripple Creek, Pueblo,
or Colorado Springs for a decade after her diary ends. Emily did
not die in a Denver hospital before 1903, nor is she (or any other
member of her family except her father) buried in Calvary, Riverside, or Fairmount cemetery in Denver. The only person named
French, Rood, or Varney buried in the Elbert cemetery was Emily's little son, M. K. French, Jr., in 1885. Emily had probably left
Denver before 1894 and married Mr. Varney elsewhere.[54]

Olive French remained in Denver until at least 1894. On June
1, 1891, at the age of fifteen, she was married to W. (William) C.
Shiner, laborer, who had lived in Jacobs addition near Fairview
from 1887 to 1889. After his marriage he worked at the G. E.
Corbin and Sons Dairy and lived on the south side of Monroe
near Main at or near the dairy. He and Ollie did not appear in the
1893 directory, and on February 14, 1894, Ollie was granted a divorce from her husband. In the 1894 directory she was listed as
"Mrs. Olive Shiner" living on the north side of Willow Street near
Main, which would be across the street from her mother's house.
She does not appear in later Denver city directories, nor in the
1900 census.[55]

Annis Rood was issued a patent for her homestead near Elbert
on February 6, 1891. On June 19, 1891, she sold the property to
H. C. Rider in Elbert. She, too, disappears from the records.[56]

Marsena French remained in Colorado, as far as we know, until
at least 1904, when he sold off part of his homestead. In 1896 he
was listed as a physician living in Denver at 1136 Tenth Avenue.
The next year, according to the directory, he was not living in
Denver and had perhaps moved back to Elbert. In 1900 he was
living in Elbert with his wife Celia, stepson Otho Firman, and son
Charles Dewitt French, now nine years old. He was not living in

Elbert when the 1910 U.S. Census was taken, nor do Elbert records show Marsena's death in that community.[57]

In 1900 Daniel T. French, now twenty-two, was living at Elbert as a boarder in the house of August Kunze and his wife, Mary, but he was not in Elbert in 1910 when the census was taken.[58]

In 1893 Chauncey, now known as Morgan C. French, sold his property at Barr City. By 1900 he was living in Pueblo, Colorado, with his wife, Tillie, aged twenty-one, from Michigan, and three children, Hazel, Chauncey, and Ellie. By 1919 he was living in Craig, Colorado, where he attracted publicity as the inventor of a sagebrush plow.[59]

The history of the diary itself is mysteriously lacking. Someone gave it to Colorado College in Colorado Springs, but the Tutt Library has no record of the diary's donor or when it was accessioned. It may have been given to the library as early as the 1890s, by Emily's sister or children. Or perhaps the donor was a stranger to the family, who had somehow come into possession of the diary and recognized its extraordinary power and its superb description of a woman's life and thoughts in 1890.

Notes

DISCOVERING EMILY

1. Elizabeth Hampsten, *Read This Only to Yourself: The Private Writings of Midwestern Women, 1880–1910* (Bloomington: Indiana University Press, 1982), pp. 48–95.

2. For various motives of diarists see Robert A. Fothergill, *Private Chronicles, A Study of English Diaries* (London: Oxford University Press, 1974); and Thomas Mallon, *A Book of One's Own: People and Their Diaries* (New York: Ticknor & Fields, 1984).

3. Colorado Census, 1885, Elbert, gives Emily's age and birthplace. In the U.S. Census, 1840, Michigan, Calhoun Co., Concord Twp., Rood was listed as a white male between twenty and thirty years old. A Denver neighbor testified he had known Rood since 1860. Testimony of Hans Streck, Estate of Morgan L. Rood, Arapahoe County (Colo.) Probate Court Records, Denver, no. 656, Jan. 16, 1882. Rood's associate in his gun shop, E. G. Owens, described Rood's life story and adventures in a newspaper interview entitled "Crack Shots of the West. Old Time hunters and their skill with the rifle." Unidentified newspaper clipping in Will C. Ferril's scrapbook, vol. 1, pp. 88–90, Western History, Denver Public Library. Rood's gun shop was at 202 Fifteenth Street, Denver. He was probably divorced from Emily's mother, because she was still alive after his second marriage and sent a silk dress to Abby, Emily's daughter born in 1871 (April 7). For Rood's marriage to Anna Bickford see *Rocky Mountain News* (Denver), Feb. 7, 1868, p. 4, c. 4. He died November 25, 1881, and was

buried in Riverside Cemetery. See "Riverside Cemetery, 1863–1908, Denver, Colorado," presented by Columbine Chapter of the Daughters of the American Revolution (Denver, 1971), copy in Denver Public Library.

4. Date of elopement (March 17); divorce decree, *Marsena H. French* v. *Emily L. French,* June 29, 1889, Denver Superior Court Records, Docket no. 11286; children in U.S. Census, 1870, Iowa, Jones Co., Anamosa, Fairview Twp., and U.S. Census, 1880, Iowa, Linn Co., Spring Grove Twp., Troy Mills; *Anamosa* (Iowa) *Eureka,* March 21, 1867, p. 3, c. 1; April 11, 1867, p. 3, c. 3; Sept. 19, 1867, p. 3, c. 2.

5. U.S. Census, 1870, Iowa, Jones Co., Anamosa, Fairview Twp.; *Anamosa Eureka,* April 28, 1870, p. 3, c. 1; May 12, 1870, p. 2, c. 7. Marsena first appears in the *Anamosa Eureka* with a claim against the county in 1866 (Sept. 13, 1866, p. 1, c. 7). On March 18, 1867, he bought the clothing store and lot on Main Street from Dr. N. G. Sales for $1,000 (Book D, Jones Co. [Iowa] records, Jones County Clerk's Office, Anamosa, Iowa), and on April 22, 1868, N. G. Sales brought suit against M. L. French and Emily L. French for default on promissory note and decree of foreclosure (references courtesy of Cathie Jackson). *Anamosa Eureka,* April 22, 1868, p. 3, c. 4. Chauncey French, perhaps Marsena's brother, appeared in the *Anamosa Eureka* on August 20, 1868, p. 3, c. 4, as delegate to the county convention, and continued to show up as an enterprising and respected man until at least 1871. In 1869 the son born to Marsena and Emily was named Morgan Chauncey. A "Myron" in the diary may have been another relative of Marsena's. Myron H. French was buried in the Fairmount Cemetery in Denver on July 15, 1906, aged fifty-one years, a year or two older than the "Myron" who turned thirty-seven in Emily's diary (March 29). "Burial Records of Fairmount Cemetery Denver Colorado 1891–1906. Copied 1949 by Mrs. W. L. Irish (Stella Potnam Irish)," Genealogy Department, Denver Public Library.

6. *Anamosa Eureka,* Oct. 13, 1870, p. 3, c. 1. Before they left Anamosa, Emily and Marsena together sold lots in Anamosa for $550 that Emily alone had bought for $150 in 1870. See Book E, Jones Co. (Iowa) Records, p. 461, and Book G, p. 345. I am indebted to Cathie Jackson for research in the Jones County records.

7. George Rosen, *The Structure of American Medical Practice, 1875–1941* (Philadelphia: University of Pennsylvania, 1943), pp. 7, 14–15, 19–23, 35–36.

8. *Storm Lake* (Iowa) *Pilot,* April 24, 1872; Dec. 11, 1872; Oct. 21, 1874; Nov. 17, 1875; Dec. 28, 1875. For Olive's birth, Colorado Census, 1885, Elbert Co.; for almost all material on the French family in Newell and Storm Lake, including items from the *Storm Lake Pilot,* my thanks to George ("Slew") Davenport who reports that the Buena Vista County courthouse at Storm Lake burned down in 1877, destroying public records.

9. Daniel's birth in *The Golden* (Colo.) *Transcript,* Oct. 12, 1877. Marsena is listed as a Golden physician in Ballenger and Richards, *Third Annual Colorado State Business Directory and Annual Register* (Denver: J. A. Blake, 1877), pp. 165–76 (hereafter cited as *Colorado Business Directory*); *Colorado Business Directory,* 1878, p. 150; *Colorado Business Directory,* 1879, p. 141. U.S. Census, 1880, Iowa, Linn Co., Spring Grove Twp., Troy Mills, lists Marsena as a physician aged forty-five, and Emily as a housewife aged thirty-seven, living with children Helen H. aged seventeen, Emily aged thirteen, M. Chauncey aged eleven, Abigail M. aged nine, Olive Esther aged four, and Daniel T. aged two.

10. Colorado Census, 1885, Elbert Co., Schedule B, lists M. K. French, Jr., aged four, under "Persons who died during the year ending May 31, 1885." A "French infant" is buried in the Elbert Cemetery (no date given) in lot 70, block 5, owned by M. H. French. Elbert Cemetery Records, Kay Merrill, Eileen Hawkins, Ruby S. Hoskins, Bonny Lillywhite, compilers, *Colorado Records & Resources,* vol. 1 (Englewood, Colo., 1981). Estate of Morgan L. Rood, Arapahoe County Probate Court Records, no. 656, Jan. 16, 1882; petition of *Emily L. French* et al. v. *Anna Rood Luedeke,* to set aside will, May 12, 1883, Register of Arapahoe County District Court, Denver, no. 6783; petition of *Emily L. French, Annis L. Rood, and Isaac M. Rood* [and John Rood] v. *Anna Rood Luedeke,* June 24, 1884, for partition of estate, Register of Arapahoe County District Court no. 7651. In Arapahoe County (Denver) Grantee–Grantor Book 44 (April–June, 1893) Emily L. French et al. were granted a court order by Anna Luedeke, record to be found in Book 851, p. 335 (but I could not locate Book 851). Very soon after Morgan Rood's death Anna Rood married Herman Luedeke, architect for Rood's house built in 1881 at Seventeenth and Glenarm streets. In the 1880s Arapahoe County encompassed what is now Denver City and County.

11. Judgment and verdict, *Emily L. French et al.* v. *Anna Rood Luedeke,*

June 24, 1884, motion to set aside and new trial denied, Arapahoe County District Court no. 6783; the Denver address of the Frenches in 1884 was 1446 South Tenth Street. *Twelfth Annual Denver City Directory* (Denver: Ballenger and Richards, 1884) (hereafter cited as *Denver City Directory*); *Colorado, New Mexico, Utah, Nevada, Wyoming, and Arizona Gazetteer and Business Directory, 1884–5* (Chicago: R. L. Polke & Co., 1889), p. 154; Colorado Census, 1885, Elbert Co.; testimony of Marsena H. French, with his Homestead Application no. 16970, filed May 11, 1885, Denver Land Office Records, RG 49, National Archives, Wash., D.C. Marsena's advertisement was in the *Elbert County Tribune* of October 15, 1885, files of the Elbert County Historical Society, Elbert County Library, Kiowa, Colo.

12. Annis L. Rood, Homestead Application no. 6155, filed May 14, 1885 (W2 NW4 Sec. 32, E2 NE4 Sec. 31 T9S R64W), final certificate no. 3155; U.S. Census, 1870, New Jersey, Atlantic Co., Hammonton. Annis's improvements included a frame house 12 x 12 feet, with a 14 x 14 foot attached kitchen, a barn, a mile and a quarter of two-wire barbed wire fence, and 10 acres ploughed. She testified that she was forty-five years old, born in Calhoun County, Michigan. On October 15, 1890, she advertised her intention of making final proof but on December 12, 1890, she was notified that the newspaper had misspelled her name as "Annie" requiring refiling in Denver and readvertising; this requirement was waived after testimony that she was crippled and obliged to be carried from place to place, as well as "wholly destitute of means and compelled to rely upon the labors of affiant's mother" (meaning Emily). Testimony with Homestead Application no. 6155, final certificate no. 3155, Feb. 6, 1891, Denver Land Office Records, RG 49.

13. Marsena H. French filed his Homestead Application no. 16970 on May 11, 1885, for S2 SW4 Sec. 29, E2 NW4 Sec. 32 T9S R64W. He filed a Timber Culture Claim application June 2, 1885, no. 2488 for N2 SW4 and S2 NW4 Sec. 29 T9S R64W, final certificate no. 182, June 13, 1894, Denver Land Office Records, RG 49.

14. Gilbert C. Fite, *The Farmers' Frontier, 1865–1900* (Albuquerque: University of New Mexico Press, 1974), pp. 124–25; Everett Dick, *Conquering the Great American Desert: Nebraska,* Nebraska State Historical Society Publications, vol. 27 ([Lincoln] 1975), pp. 120–21.

15. Testimony of Marsena H. French, June 11, 1894, for Timber Culture

Claim; Emily L. French of Elbert County, Last Will and Testament, Annis L. Rood, Last Will and Testament, both executed December 27, 1888, witnessed by John C. and Mrs. John C. Currier, and filed with Elbert County Records, Kiowa, Colo., Book 13, p. 431; *Marsena H. French v. Emily L. French,* divorce decree, June 29, 1889, Denver Superior Court Docket no. 11286, Denver City-County Building; the filing and proceedings are not among the divorce records in the Denver City-County Building; the divorce decree shows no custody award of the minor children to either parent—was Emily hiding Olive and Dannie in Denver (January 17) because Marsena had grounds for custody of them? John Currier was a carpenter and laborer for J. H. Nicholas, a well-known Denver landscape gardener on Hunt Street and Third Avenue. John C. and Anna Currier were witnesses to Emily's will of December 28, 1888, signed in Elbert.

16. "M. K. French, Jr.," aged four, died of accidental poisoning early in 1885. Colorado Census, 1885, Elbert Co., Schedule B, "Persons who died during year ending May 31, 1885." M. H. French owned a lot in the cemetery where a French infant was buried (no dates). Elbert Cemetery Records, *Colorado Records & Resources,* vol. 1. A "little boy named French" was listed by Ethel Rae Corbett as the first person buried in the Elbert Cemetery; see Corbett, *Western Pioneer Days: Biographies and Genealogies of Early Settlers with History of Elbert County, Colorado* (Denver: n.p., 1974), p. 213. For Marsena's new family see U.S. Census, 1900, Colorado, Elbert Co.

17. Petition of Anna Rood, Dec. 31, 1881. Estate of Morgan L. Rood, Arapahoe County Probate Court Records; testimony of Abigail M. Mellor and Chauncey M. French, June 11, 1894, in support of Marsena H. French's Timber Culture Claim. Addie Quick was Dan Larkin's sister. She was listed as "Addie L. Larkin" in the *Denver City Directory* for 1890 living at 234 Thurman Street, Jerome Park, the home of F. Quick, lather.

18. Description of Elbert in *Colorado Business Directory,* 1890.

19. Corbett, *Western Pioneer Days,* p. 213; Emily had a cold in January, then caught "La Grippe" or "catarrhal fever," an epidemic of dangerous influenza that was killing people worldwide. *Rocky Mountain News,* Jan. 2, p. 4, c. 6; Jan. 5, p. 1, c. 2; Jan. 6, p. 1, c. 3.

20. Among the celebrations were Decoration Day, May 30, with a downtown parade of old soldiers, and a ceremony at Riverside Cemetery

where Emily put flowers on her father's grave. She does not mention that a woman was killed and several other persons injured by runaway horses dragging buggies and wagons over gravestones and through the crowds. *Rocky Mountain News,* May 31, p. 2, c. 1–2. On the Fourth of July there was a three-hour parade downtown, and dedication of the new capitol, a free barbecue for 60,000 people in one park, and fireworks at night in another park, all of which Emily and the children attended. Emily and the newspaper account do not agree about parks where these events took place. *Rocky Mountain News,* July 5, p. 5, c. 1. Emily's free picnic on July 20 at Crystal Lake escaped notice in the newspaper. A John Lawson listed in the 1890 *Denver City Directory* as a miner living in the rear of a boarding house at 10 Golden Avenue west of the Platte River was the most likely John Lawson to have been Emily's lover; Denver directories before and after 1890 list two or three men named John Lawson at various locations and in various jobs.

21. John Moncrieff, an elderly Scottish real estate agent, sold Emily lot 22, block 4, in Fairview for $500; Emily traded Moncrieff lots 42 and 43, block 18, in South University Place, subject to trust deeds of $20 and $75, respectively. *Rocky Mountain News,* April 24, p. 8, c. 3. Emily did not take out a building permit; no permit appears under her name in the applications for Denver building permits, April–May 1890, City and County of Denver Building Department, nor does her property appear in the tax records for 1890, Assessor's Office, Denver City-County Building. Joe Phillips, abstracter who helped me in the Denver County Clerk's Office, assures me that the abstract on Emily's property no longer exists. On July 17, the date Emily started to look for work, the *Rocky Mountain News* want ads listed only six positions for houseworkers.

22. See section introduction to "Dake—The Mountains in Summer."

23. One of Emily's employers was the wife of Dr. N. G. Burnham who sat in Box C at the Fifteenth Street Theater on "society night." *Rocky Mountain News,* Nov. 18, p. 7, c. 5. Annis's lawsuit was *The People* v. *Chancy* [sic] *French* for grand larceny, December 11, 1889, Fourth Judicial District Court, Elbert County, Grand Docket no. 132, p. 90, defendant arraigned and pleads not guilty; jury verdict not guilty. *The People* v. *M. H. French,* accessory to grand larceny, continued from

December 1889, Grand Docket no. 131, p. 89; *nol. pros.* entered and accepted by court.

24. J. C. Smiley wrote in his *History of Denver with Outlines of the Earlier History of the Rocky Mountain Country, edited for the Denver Times by Jerome C. Smiley* (Denver: *Times-Sun* Publishing Co., 1901), p. 777, "there is wretchedness and misery in the city, but so much of it is directly associated with wantoness and other vice." The dean of Denver's Episcopal Cathedral preached in 1890 that the poor should be given sympathy instead of money, for money would encourage their laziness. *Rocky Mountain News,* Nov. 28, 1890, p. 9, c. 3–4. For examples of "deserving poor," see *Rocky Mountain News,* Nov. 13, p. 8, c. 1, Nov. 23, p. 24, c. 1–5. The Salvation Army had been organized in Colorado in 1887; it had fifty workers in 1890, few of them women. *Rocky Mountain News,* July 28, 1890, p. 5, c. 1.

25. Barbara Welter, "The Cult of True Womanhood," in *Women and Womanhood in America,* ed. Ronald W. Hogeland (Lexington, Mass.: D. C. Heath, 1973), pp. 103–13; a fine interpretation of this Victorian ideal as it applied to California women is Robert L. Griswold's *Family and Divorce in California, 1850–1890: Victorian Illusions and Everyday Realities* (Albany: State University of New York Press, 1982), pp. 39–46.

26. Griswold, *Family and Divorce in California,* pp. 28, 170–79; William L. O'Neill, "Divorce as a Moral Issue: A Hundred Years of Controversy," in *Remember the Ladies: New Perspectives on Women in American History. Essays in Honor of Nelson Manfred Blake,* ed. Carol V. R. George (Syracuse: Syracuse University Press, 1975), p. 130, sees divorce as a safety valve for unhappy marriages and essential to the companionate ideal of marriage.

27. The extant record of Emily's divorce consists of the decree only, without stated alimony or child support; nor does the diary indicate any financial help from Marsena for Emily or the children; U.S. Commissioner of Labor, *Marriage and Divorce in the United States, 1867 to 1886,* First Special Report (Washington, D.C.: Government Printing Office, 1897), pp. 29, 91, 140, 144, 152, 169–71; Nathan Allen's article in *North American Review* cited by O'Neill, "Divorce as a Moral Issue," p. 133; Griswold, *Family and Divorce in California,* pp. 23–31; William L. O'Neill, *Divorce in the Progressive Era* (New Haven and London: Yale University Press, 1967), pp. 19–23; Joyce D. Good-

friend, "The Struggle for Survival: Widows in Denver, Colorado, 1880–1912," paper presented at Western History Association meeting, Phoenix, Ariz., 1982, typescript graciously loaned to me by the author.

28. *Rocky Mountain News,* June 1, 1890, p. 18, c. 6; July 20, 1890, p. 22, c. 1–2.

29. Alice Kessler-Harris, *Women Have Always Worked: A Historical Overview* (Old Westbury, N.Y.: McGraw-Hill, 1981), pp. 79–87.

30. *Rocky Mountain News,* March 16, p. 12, c. 4; Goodfriend, "The Struggle for Survival."

31. Mary Murphy, "Woman's Work in a Man's World," *The Speculator,* Butte Historical Society (Winter 1984): 21, finds evidence that store owners and school administrators of Butte, Montana, in 1900 did not hire older women because of possible conflict with employees' responsibilities to children or spouses; want ads for women workers in the *Rocky Mountain News* of 1890 usually specify "young woman," "good girl," or "woman under 45" (see, for instance, Aug. 29, p. 9, c. 6).

32. Griswold, *Family and Divorce in California,* pp. 51–60.

33. A typical book company advertised in the *Rocky Mountain News,* Jan. 2, 1890, p. 2, c. 3. The company charged a dollar for an "outfit" which was refunded when the agent had sold ten copies. No capital was required, and books were delivered anywhere at the expense of the company. The book to be sold was *Heroes of the Dark Continent: or, How Stanley Found Emir Pasha* (this is the same book Emily sold, but not through the same company). For taking in boarders, see Goodfriend, "The Struggle for Survival"; Kessler-Harris, *Women Have Always Worked,* pp. 48–49.

34. Joseph G. Rayback, *History of American Labor* (New York: Macmillan, 1963), pp. 92–103; Grace Abbott, *The Child and the State,* vol. 1 (Chicago: University of Chicago Press, 1938), pp. 279–81.

ELBERT: THE PLAINS IN WINTER

35. Elbert, in *Colorado Business Directory,* 1890; Frank Hall, *History of the State of Colorado, 1858–1890,* vol. 4 (Chicago: Blakely Printing Co., 1895), pp. 127–28.

36. Corbett, *Western Pioneer Days,* pp. 211–12; U.S. Census, Colorado, 1910.

37. Corbett, *Western Pioneer Days,* pp. 20–21.

38. Ibid., pp. 211–12; a flood at Elbert in 1935 destroyed the railway tracks, depot, and so on, and service was abandoned.

DENVER: THE CITY IN SPRING

39. *Rocky Mountain News,* May 18, 1890, p. 1, c. 4–7; Smiley, *History of Denver,* pp. 483–85; Carl Ubbelohde, Maxine Benson, and Duane A. Smith, *A Colorado History: Revised Centennial Edition* (Boulder: Pruett Publishing, 1976), pp. 203–7. U.S. Census figures and those of the 1890 *Denver Business Directory* do not agree. The latter showed the population of Denver as 157,098, an increase of 40 percent in just one year (compare the national average yearly population increase at 26 percent).

40. *Rocky Mountain News,* Jan. 5, 1890, p. 9, c. 4–6 (construction); Feb. 28, p. 1, c. 7 (Patti); March 30, p. 16, c. 1–8 (electric railways); May 24, p. 4, c. 5 (entertainments); May 29, p. 6, c. 6–9 (balloons); May 31, p. 2, c. 1–2 (Decoration Day); June 28, p. 6, c. 1 (picnics); July 5, p. 5, c. 1 (Fourth of July); July 5, p. 9, c. 1–5 (parade); Aug. 29, p. 5, c. 2 (Barrymore—but not Lionel, Ethel, or John); Smiley, *History of Denver,* pp. 456, 484–85, 910; Stephen J. Leonard, "Denver's Foreign Born Immigrants 1859–1900," Ph.D. diss. Claremont Graduate School, 1971; Andrew Morrison, *The City of Denver and State of Colorado* (Saint Louis: Englehardt Series, 1890), pp. 16–18; Lyle W. Dorsett, *The Queen City: A History of Denver* (Boulder: Pruett Publishing, 1977), p. 92.

41. Lawrence H. Larsen, *The Urban West at the End of the Frontier* (Lawrence: Regents Press of Kansas, 1978); *Rocky Mountain News,* July 16, 1890, p. 3, c. 5–8 (Tent Town); Oct. 4, p. 7, c. 1 (Platte River); Nov. 23, p. 25, c. 3 (saloons).

42. Dan Larkin's sister, Addie Quick was the intermediary to whom Emily sent letters for her children early in 1890. She lived at 234 Thurman Street, near Jerome Park in South Denver, at the home of F. Quick, lather, perhaps a relative of the Charley Quick mentioned in the diary whom Addie stole from his wife (May 4). Her real name was Addie L. Larkin, and so she was shown in the *Denver City Directory* from 1889 to 1894.

43. For Emily's neighbors, see the *Denver City Directory* for 1890.

44. Emily bought her Fairview lot for $500 from John Moncrieff (*Rocky*

Mountain News April 24, 1890, p. 8, c. 3). The legal description of Fairview was S2 NE4 Sec. 5 T4S R68W, Plat Book no. 1, Records Room, Denver County Clerk's Office; the old street names are shown on *The City of Denver,* a map published in about 1885 by H. L. Thayer, copy in Stephen H. Hart Library, Colorado Historical Society, Denver.

DAKE: THE MOUNTAINS IN SUMMER

45. For a description of Buffalo Creek Park, see *Rocky Mountain News,* July 29, 1890, p. 13, c. 4; for Denver and South Park Railway, see Hall, *History of the State of Colorado* vol. 4, pp. 53–54; and M. C. Poor, *Denver, South Park & Pacific* (Denver: Rocky Mountain Ralroad Club, c. 1949), pp. 150, 422. Emily followed the original stage route between Denver and South Park from Morrison up Bear Creek, crossing a divide to Turkey Creek; up that stream to Elk Creek and over a high divide to the north fork of the South Platte; up the Platte River to its head in Kenosha Pass. Hall, *History of The State of Colorado,* vol. 4, p. 267.

46. R. H. Kindig, E. J. Haley, M. C. Poor, *Pictorial Supplement to Denver, South Park & Pacific* (Denver: Rocky Mountain Railroad Club, 1959), p. 275. For Grant, see Poor, *Denver, South Park & Pacific,* supplement, p. 275; *Colorado Business Directory,* 1890.

47. For Webster, see Hall, *History of the State of Colorado,* vol. 4, p. 267; Poor, *Denver, South Park & Pacific,* p. 150, 153 (photo); *Colorado Business Directory,* 1890.

48. *Colorado Business Directory,* 1890, 1891; verbal information from James A. O'Keefe, chief draftsman of the Colorado and Southern Railway, Denver, April 17, 1940, in the Stephen H. Hart Library, Colorado Historical Society; for Alvin C. Dake and his wife Charlotte, see obituaries, *Denver Times,* Sept. 5, 1902, p. 2, c. 1; and *Denver Post,* May 28, 1937, p. 3.

DENVER: THE CITY IN AUTUMN

49. Smiley, *History of Denver,* pp. 485–86, 913–17, *Denver City Directory,* 1890; *Rocky Mountain News,* Nov. 13, 1890, p. 5, c. 3.

50. *Denver City Directory,* 1890.

51. Smiley, *History of Denver,* pp. 637, 728; Morrison, *The City of Denver,* p. 31; *Denver City Directory,* 1890.

52. Smiley, *History of Denver,* pp. 913–17.

EPILOGUE

53. Marsena H. French, Homestead Application no. 6131 (S2 SW4 Sec. 29, E2 NW4 Sec. 32 T9S R64W), canceled; Marsena H. French, Homestead Application no. 16970, final certificate no. 3879, Feb. 27, 1895, Denver Land Office Records, RG 49.

54. "The City of Denver Register of Deaths, Oct., 1889 to March 1891," Colorado State Archives, Denver, with permission of Denver Department of Health and Hospitals; "Calvary Cemetery, Denver, Colorado," burial records copied by Sadie L. George in 1945, copy in Denver Public Library; "Riverside Cemetery, 1863–1908, Denver, Colorado"; Elbert Co. death records to 1900, Elbert County Records, Kiowa, Colo.; "Burial Records of Fairmount Cemetery Denver Colorado 1891–1906"; Elbert County Cemetery Records, *Colorado Records & Resources,* vol. 1. Between 1891 and 1893 the *Denver City Directory* listed six men named Varney: Edgar D., principal of the Bryant School; Hiram, photographer and printer; Nathan, bookkeeper; Patrick, carpenter; Fred W., assayer; Charles W., stereotyper; in 1894 only Hiram and Nathan were listed. As Emily's marriage is not recorded in Denver (Denver Marriage Records, Sept. 26, 1867 to Jan. 26, 1906, Book 900, Colorado State Archives), she may have met her husband elsewhere.

55. Olive and Shiner were married by the Reverend L. J. John, witnessed by George J. Corbin, Fred G. Erdman, Olive Maud Rose, and Lizzie Jessamine Rose. Denver Marriage Records, Sept. 26, 1867 to Jan. 26, 1906. p. 74, Colorado State Archives. See Divorce Decree no. 20724, Arapahoe County Court Records; *Denver City Directory,* 1894, p. 903.

56. Annis L. Rood, Homestead Application no. 6155, final certificate no. 3155, Denver Land Office Records; Annis L. Rood to H. C. Rider, Warranty Deed, June 19, 1891, Elbert County Records, Book 11, p. 597.

57. Marsena H. French to Jacob Epler, Warranty Deed, April 22, 1904, Elbert County Records, Book 37, p. 446; *Denver City Directory,* 1896; U.S. Census, 1900, Colorado, Elbert Co.

58. U.S. Census, 1900, Colorado, Elbert Co.

59. Morgan C. French to David Schoonmaker, Trust Deed for property at Barr City, June 17, 1893, Arapahoe County Records, Book 44, p. 460; U.S. Census, 1900, Colorado, Pueblo Co.; *Denver City Directories*, 1888–1893; *Colorado Business Directory*, 1916; *The French Plow, Town and Mfg. Company. Main Office Craig, Colorado. Denver office 314 Colorado Bldg.*, pamphlet, Western History, Denver Public Library; *Colorado Business Directory* for 1920 shows the French Plow, Town and Mfg. Co. under R. A. Kellog, and does not mention French.

Index